Seen/Unseen

New Perspectives on the Civil War Era

Seen/Unseen

Hidden Lives in a Community of Enslaved Georgians

Written and edited by

Christopher R. Lawton

Laura E. Nelson

Randy L. Reid

The University of Georgia Press

ATHENS

© 2021 by the University of Georgia Press
Athens, Georgia 30602
www.ugapress.org
All rights reserved
Set in 10/13 ITC New Baskerville Std
by Kaelin Chappell Broaddus

Most University of Georgia Press titles are
available from popular e-book vendors.

Printed digitally

Library of Congress Cataloging-in-Publication Data

Names: Lamar, J. B. (John Basil), 1812–1862. | Cobb, Howell, 1815–
1868. | Cobb, Mary Ann Lamar, 1818–1889. | Lawton, Christopher
R., 1972– editor, author. | Nelson, Laura E., 1993– editor, author.
| Reid, Randy L., 1955– editor, author. | Hargrett Library.
Title: Seen/unseen : hidden lives in a community of enslaved Georgians / written
and edited by Christopher R. Lawton, Laura E. Nelson, Randy L. Reid.
Other titles: New Perspectives on the Civil War Era.
Description: Athens : The University of Georgia Press, 2021. | Series: New perspectives
on the Civil War era | Includes bibliographical references and index.
Identifiers: LCCN 2020030540 | ISBN 9780820358970 (hardback) | ISBN
9780820358987 (paperback) | ISBN 9780820358963 (ebook)
Subjects: LCSH: Mills, Aggy Carter, approximately 1826–approximately 1901.
Lamar, J. B. (John Basil), 1812–1862—Correspondence. | Cobb, Howell,
1815–1868—Correspondence. | Cobb, Mary Ann Lamar, 1818–1889—
Correspondence. | African Americans—Georgia—Social conditions—19th
century—Sources. | Slaves—Georgia—Social conditions—19th century—
Sources. | African Americans—Georgia—History—19th century—Sources.
| Plantation life—Georgia—History—19th century—Sources.
Classification: LCC E185.93.G4 S44 2021 | DDC 306.3/620975809034—dc23
LC record available at https://lccn.loc.gov/2020030540

Here's one delusion: That we can escape slavery. We can't. Its scars will never fade.

—COLSON WHITEHEAD, *The Underground Railroad*

Contents

Cobb-Lamar plantations in Georgia, ca. 1835–1865.
Map by Larry Tenner.

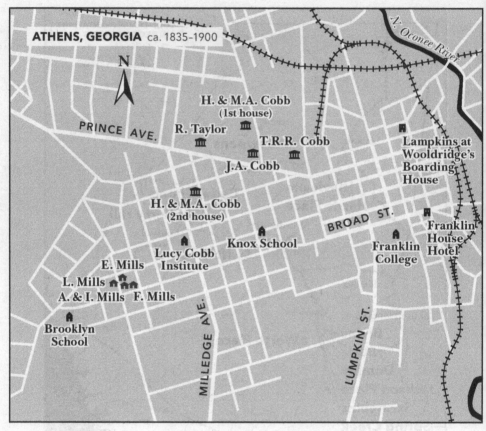

Athens, Georgia, ca. 1835–1900.
Map by Larry Tenner.

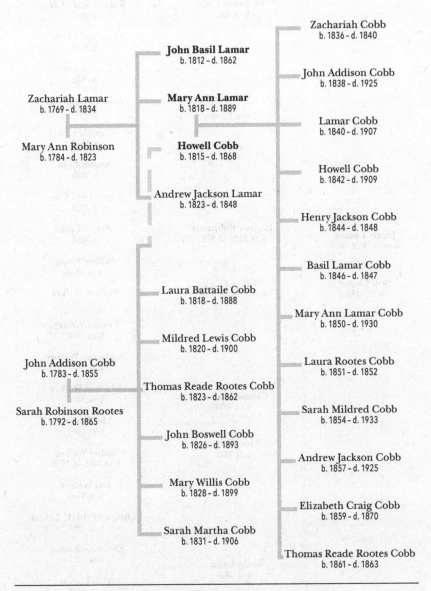

Zachariah Lamar
b. 1769 - d. 1834

Mary Ann Robinson
b. 1784 - d. 1823

John Basil Lamar
b. 1812 - d. 1862

Mary Ann Lamar
b. 1818 - d. 1889

Howell Cobb
b. 1815 - d. 1868

Andrew Jackson Lamar
b. 1823 - d. 1848

John Addison Cobb
b. 1783 - d. 1855

Sarah Robinson Rootes
b. 1792 - d. 1865

Laura Battaile Cobb
b. 1818 - d. 1888

Mildred Lewis Cobb
b. 1820 - d. 1900

Thomas Reade Rootes Cobb
b. 1823 - d. 1862

John Boswell Cobb
b. 1826 - d. 1893

Mary Willis Cobb
b. 1828 - d. 1899

Sarah Martha Cobb
b. 1831 - d. 1906

Zachariah Cobb
b. 1836 - d. 1840

John Addison Cobb
b. 1838 - d. 1925

Lamar Cobb
b. 1840 - d. 1907

Howell Cobb
b. 1842 - d. 1909

Henry Jackson Cobb
b. 1844 - d. 1848

Basil Lamar Cobb
b. 1846 - d. 1847

Mary Ann Lamar Cobb
b. 1850 - d. 1930

Laura Rootes Cobb
b. 1851 - d. 1852

Sarah Mildred Cobb
b. 1854 - d. 1933

Andrew Jackson Cobb
b. 1857 - d. 1925

Elizabeth Craig Cobb
b. 1859 - d. 1870

Thomas Reade Rootes Cobb
b. 1861 - d. 1863

Howell Cobb, Mary Ann (Lamar) Cobb,
and John B. Lamar

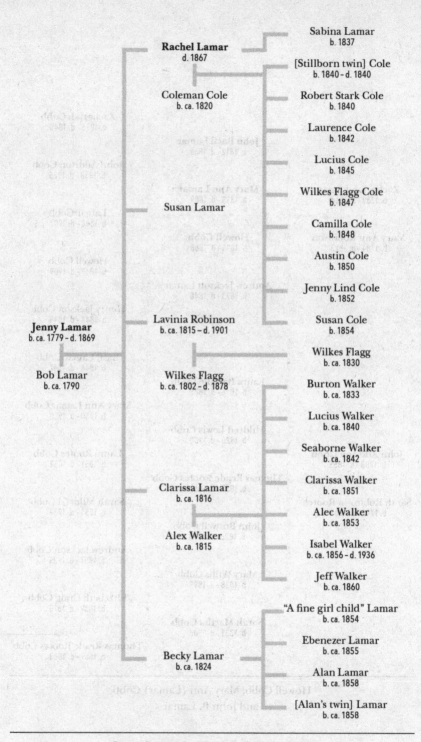

Jenny Lamar and Rachel (Lamar) Cole

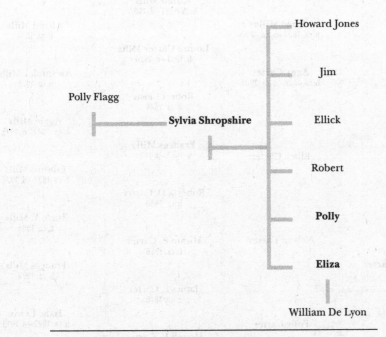

Polly Flagg ——— Sylvia Shropshire

Howard Jones

Jim

Ellick

Robert

Polly

Eliza

William De Lyon

Sylvia, Polly, and Eliza

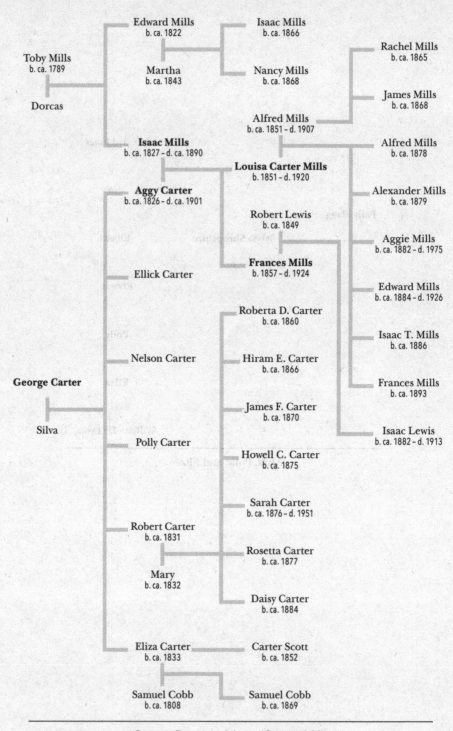

Toby Mills
b. ca. 1789

Dorcas

Edward Mills
b. ca. 1822

Martha
b. ca. 1843

Isaac Mills
b. ca. 1866

Nancy Mills
b. ca. 1868

Rachel Mills
b. ca. 1865

James Mills
b. ca. 1868

Alfred Mills
b. ca. 1851 - d. 1907

Isaac Mills
b. ca. 1827 - d. ca. 1890

Louisa Carter Mills
b. 1851 - d. 1920

Alfred Mills
b. ca. 1878

Aggy Carter
b. ca. 1826 - d. ca. 1901

Alexander Mills
b. ca. 1879

Robert Lewis
b. ca. 1849

Aggie Mills
b. ca. 1882 - d. 1975

Ellick Carter

Frances Mills
b. 1857 - d. 1924

Edward Mills
b. ca. 1884 - d. 1926

Roberta D. Carter
b. ca. 1860

Isaac T. Mills
b. ca. 1886

Nelson Carter

Hiram E. Carter
b. ca. 1866

Frances Mills
b. ca. 1893

George Carter

James F. Carter
b. ca. 1870

Isaac Lewis
b. ca. 1882 - d. 1913

Silva

Polly Carter

Howell C. Carter
b. ca. 1875

Sarah Carter
b. ca. 1876 - d. 1951

Robert Carter
b. ca. 1831

Rosetta Carter
b. ca. 1877

Mary
b. ca. 1832

Daisy Carter
b. ca. 1884

Eliza Carter
b. ca. 1833

Carter Scott
b. ca. 1852

Samuel Cobb
b. ca. 1808

Samuel Cobb
b. ca. 1869

George Carter and Aggy (Carter) Mills

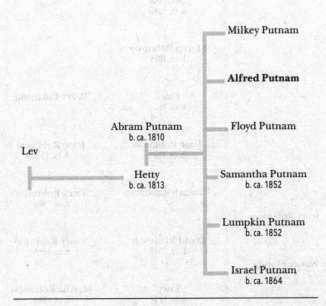

Milkey Putnam

Alfred Putnam

Floyd Putnam

Abram Putnam
b. ca. 1810

Lev

Hetty
b. ca. 1813

Samantha Putnam
b. ca. 1852

Lumpkin Putnam
b. ca. 1852

Israel Putnam
b. ca. 1864

Alfred Putnam

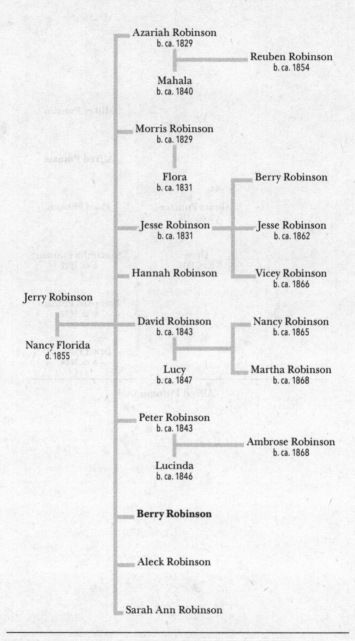

Azariah Robinson
b. ca. 1829

Reuben Robinson
b. ca. 1854

Mahala
b. ca. 1840

Morris Robinson
b. ca. 1829

Flora
b. ca. 1831

Berry Robinson

Jesse Robinson
b. ca. 1831

Jesse Robinson
b. ca. 1862

Hannah Robinson

Vicey Robinson
b. ca. 1866

Jerry Robinson

David Robinson
b. ca. 1843

Nancy Robinson
b. ca. 1865

Nancy Florida
d. 1855

Lucy
b. ca. 1847

Martha Robinson
b. ca. 1868

Peter Robinson
b. ca. 1843

Ambrose Robinson
b. ca. 1868

Lucinda
b. ca. 1846

Berry Robinson

Aleck Robinson

Sarah Ann Robinson

Berry Robinson

Seen/Unseen

Prologue

THE GHOSTS OF THE ENSLAVED HAUNT US STILL. We live in a nation that has yet to come to terms with its original sin, where the past has not ceased to corrode the present. Those who were kept voiceless murmur in the distance, waiting to be heard, just out of earshot but at a frequency that torments our collective sense of what it means to be American.

This book is an attempt to allow one community of the enslaved to be seen and have their voices heard. To research and write it was to sit quietly in the presence of Bob, George, Sylvia, Rachel, Polly, Alfred, Berry, Aggy, and hundreds of other people owned by the Cobb-Lamar family and try to decipher what they had to say. It was to reckon with their anguish over having only so many days on earth and being forced to spend them in bondage. It was also to come to see that they were, in many ways, more fortunate than countless others possessed as unfree property in a country founded on the ideals of freedom and natural rights.

Those ideals allowed Mary Ann Lamar, her elder brother John Basil Lamar, and her husband Howell Cobb to build a veritable empire on the forced labor of others. Mary Ann and John B. had inherited a fortune in land and enslaved people upon the death of their father, Zachariah, in 1834. At sixteen and twenty-two, respectively, they became two of the wealthiest people in Georgia. Mary Ann's marriage to nineteen-year-old Howell the following year combined their resources with his burgeoning political acumen. Together they became one of the most socially and politically powerful southern families of the antebellum decades. The series of plantations undergirding their wealth and prominence also made possible a certain level of security for the enslaved laborers who sustained them. The majority of people the Cobb-Lamars held in bondage were infrequently sold, seldom divided from their families on a permanent basis, and possessed the agency to appeal to their owners when confronted with abuse. To be sure, the surviving documents demonstrate that all were scarred to some degree by separations and mental or physical violence. Yet small mercy that it may be, they also lived within an interconnected and relatively stable family and community network that spanned the state. They were sustained by what Frederick Douglass called "the kindred tie," joined to parents and grandparents, siblings, aunts and uncles, and a broad web of friends and acquaintances who knew one another and sought as best they could to keep each other relatively close and relatively safe.[1]

Our ability to glimpse the world made by this community of enslaved people comes from the unique circumstances of Mary Ann, Howell, and John B.'s lives. These circumstances required the maintenance of a complex correspondence that dealt with all aspects of family, business, and political matters. Because their lives were completely dependent on the people they owned, the enslaved appear constantly as actors, both minor and major, in the paper trail they left behind.

The Cobb-Lamar family archive, now housed at the University of Georgia Libraries, is built largely around three people, connected to hundreds of correspondents, comprising nearly ninety thousand documents, totaling several hundred thousand pages covered by millions and millions of words. *Seen/Unseen: Hidden Lives in a Community of Enslaved Georgians* is an attempt at using those materials to rebalance the historical record. It is the result of three historians working across five years, sifting through the paper and ink that was left behind to find several dozen enslaved people and tell only a fraction of the lives of some of them. It is a suggestion that a new lens turned on old sources can yield new evidence and reintroduce the stories of those whose names and lives once seemed lost forever.

The chronological span, geographic reach, and expansive scope of subjects addressed in the library archive make it one of the most extensive collections of materials related to nineteenth-century American life. Yet the virtues of having such a range of documentary evidence necessitated editorial decisions about which documents to incorporate and how to incorporate them into a volume of this size. This book began as a broad social history woven together from data pertaining to the general experiences of the hundreds of people the Cobb-Lamar family enslaved. As we wrote, however, we realized that delving more deeply into the most compelling accounts of some enslaved people might tell as much as, and in some ways tell far more than, a historical account based on a broad amalgamation of evidence. To tell their stories, then, we have pared down family letters to include only those portions that reveal the interior lives of our actors or shed light on their experiences.

Our primary objective in editing documents for this volume was to let the letter writers speak in their own voices. For clarity, we inserted periods

---

1. Frederick Douglass, *My Bondage and My Freedom*, with an introduction by Philip S. Foner (New York: Dover Publications, 1969), 177.

or commas where correspondents employed frequent dashes or no punc-
tuation at all to help readers follow the flow of the documents. On those
rare occasions when a word was unreadable, we inserted brackets either
noting illegibility or suggesting what we believed the author intended it to
be. Brackets were also inserted to note when a damaged portion of a document was indecipherable. If an author accidentally wrote the same word
twice, we omitted the error. Mary Ann had a habit of beginning a quotation without punctuating its close, so we inserted final quotation marks in
the appropriate places. We added ellipses within documents wherever we
have dropped text. Unless otherwise noted, all correspondence included
in this volume comes from the Howell Cobb Family Papers at the Hargrett
Rare Book and Manuscript Library at the University of Georgia.

Readers can find the primary source material contained in this book,
as well as additional documents that informed our understanding of this
enslaved community, on an accompanying website. Search for this book
on www.ugapress.org for links to this digital material.

The breadth of the family's acquaintance meant that they mentioned
numerous people in their correspondence, but we have included footnotes identifying only those individuals crucial to the narrative. Most important, we did not use the term *sic* to denote misspelled words. This
decision was crucial. Literacy was a valuable commodity in the mid-
nineteenth-century South and an especially hard-won prize for those who
lacked formal schooling. We believe that allowing phonetic spellings to
stand without editorial intrusions reveals a world of information about
the specific letter writer in the specific moment in which they wrote. To
edit away what modern readers would view as misspellings would be to
conceal the time and mental effort it took for some of our correspondents to participate in this letter-writing network.

While the focus of this volume was always intended to be the enslaved,
their actions and motivations were inextricably linked to those who enslaved them. Mary Ann, Howell, and John B. amassed far-reaching properties and hundreds of enslaved human beings, which they wove into
a proto-corporate infrastructure that functioned on its ability to move
goods and information along formal and informal pathways that spanned
the state. The correspondence that simultaneously upheld this network
and makes it knowable exists only because of what they built and chose
to preserve. To that end, it is important to note that no one of the Cobb
or Lamar lines ever referred to themselves as belonging to the collective "Cobb-Lamar" family. We, however, consistently use "Cobb-Lamar"
throughout this volume to make clear the highly complex and insepara-
ble familial and financial bonds that joined together Mary Ann, Howell,

and John B. Indeed, many of the people held in bondage by the family never knew which family member was their legal owner.

Chapter 1, then, is an exploration of the lives of Mary Ann, Howell, and John B. in order to make visible the underlying structures that supported them. It is not intended as a celebration of their wealth and power but is rather an attempt to establish the historical context for understanding the lives of those they held in bondage. Chapter 2 introduces many of those whose stories are the focus of this volume. It moves beyond the surface of the Cobb-Lamars' world to encounter the individuals whose constant labor behind the scenes made it all possible. Moreover, it explores the ways in which the enslaved not only recognized the network they had built but also attempted to manipulate its functions to make their lives and the lives of their families better. While those acts of manipulation sometimes resulted in the desired outcomes, they oftentimes provoked pushback from their frustrated owners. Chapter 3 explores the instances in which this cycle of manipulation escalated into outright resistance. The enslaved existed in a treacherous position between negotiating to improve their own lives and raising the ire of those who held them in bondage. The most successful in maneuvering through these hazards was a young enslaved woman named Aggy Carter, whom Mary Ann relied on and trusted more than any other. Chapter 4 delves deeply into Aggy's life in slavery and freedom, exploring the ways in which she protected herself and her children after carefully observing the successes and failures of other enslaved individuals who were moved into and out of the household.

To encounter the archival record of the lives of Aggy and others who labored, manipulated and resisted, and succeeded and failed is to watch slavery revealed as slow, ceaseless waves inflicting devastating psychological damage. It was a morally repugnant institution that diminished or destroyed all it touched. Aggy and hundreds of other people the Cobb-Lamars enslaved lived as a part of a remarkable community that sustained them but exacted a terrible cost. They spent every day forced to navigate a maze designed for the benefit of those who enslaved them, never able to breathe fully or deeply because every waking moment was a struggle to protect themselves and their families. Yet the necessity of relating their daily struggles and the price they paid should not inadvertently blot out our ability to also see the prosaic and commonplace activities that made up the majority of their lives. Like most human beings before or since, they built meaningful existences out of countless hours spent eating, sleeping, working, feeling, communing with others, pondering the past, and dreaming about the future.

CHAPTER 1
"Gilded Trappings"

THE STORY OF THE ENSLAVED COMMUNITY at the center of this book began to take shape with the marriage of Mary Ann Lamar and Howell Cobb in 1835. The young newlyweds came to their union, as did so many of their position, with a deep awareness of their families' pasts and broad dreams about what the combination might mean for the future. Unlike the people they held in bondage, Mary Ann, John B., and Howell had the good fortune to be born to great wealth. Their ability to build an economic and political empire that reached across Georgia and to the highest corridors of national power rested on what John B. called the "gilded trappings" their parents had created.[1] In addition to their inheritances, each of the three possessed complementary talents that, when woven together, enabled them to embrace and thrive in an exuberant age of American expansion. At its height, the empire they built encompassed more than twenty thousand acres of prime plantation lands. The coerced labor of hundreds of enslaved human beings, however, underpinned all that they achieved.

Mary Ann's and John B.'s father, Zachariah Lamar, came to Georgia from South Carolina in the early 1800s and subsequently built a vast empire of land and enslaved people. Following the death of his wife, Mary Ann Robinson Lamar, in 1823, he labored to prepare his three young children for the wealth and responsibilities they would one day inherit. John B., the eldest, had been a sensitive youth with a passion for literature, who feared that his failures in matters of the heart would lead to his one day being "found dead leaning against one of my shady sycamores, with Lord Byron in my hand."[2] Zachariah had chided him as a young

---

1. John B. Lamar to Mary Ann Lamar, undated manuscript.
2. John B. Lamar to Mary Ann Cobb, June 11, 1835.

man for being "lazy" and "ease loving."[3] Yet by the time his father's health
began to fail in the early 1830s, John B. had begun administering the
family's plantations, dealing with overseers, supervising the supplies of
food and clothing for the enslaved, and handling other aspects of the
family's holdings. Likewise, Mary Ann, the middle child, had been a shy
teenager with a tendency to depression that grew more pronounced as
she grew older. John B. pleaded with her "for Gods sake & your brothers
sake [to] *talk more*," so that she might make for herself "a character and
name for something besides wealth."[4] In her mother's absence, however,
she was taught to act as mistress of their Milledgeville home and acquire
both the finer social graces and the skills needed for the management of
enslaved domestic servants.[5] Andrew Jackson, the youngest child, escaped
much of this instruction as he was still a small boy when Zachariah died
in October 1834. The three Lamar children inherited an immense estate
of plantations, stocks and bonds, and hundreds of human beings. None
of Zachariah's heirs questioned their right to a third of their father's empire, and none questioned their right to inherit enslaved people and control their lives.

Howell's family had migrated to Georgia from North Carolina following the American Revolution. Although his grandfather had been forced
to declare bankruptcy, his father, John Addison Cobb, built a fortune in
land and enslaved people and parlayed it into a political career in Louisville, the state capital from 1796 to 1806. By the 1820s, the family had
settled in Athens, and John Addison embarked on a speculative venture
to develop a neighborhood on the northwest edge of town for the rising middle class. Despite his interest in land speculation and entrepre-
neurial ventures, John Addison remained a plantation owner. He and
his wife, Sarah, reared their seven children, Howell, Laura, Mildred,
Thomas, John, Mary Willis, and Sarah, to inherit the role. Howell's process of learning mastery over the enslaved began during his formative
years at the Cherry Hill Plantation, but this continued even after the family moved to Athens with nearly a dozen enslaved household servants. He

---

3. John B. Lamar to Mary Ann Cobb, March 31, 1856.

4. John B. Lamar to Mary Ann Lamar, undated manuscript.

5. We use "mistress" throughout this volume in the same manner as the historian Stephanie Jones-Rogers, who employs the term to communicate a specific subset of elite white
women who possessed "capital," held "dominion" equal to their husbands over the enslaved,
and exercised the authority "to teach enslaved people the skills necessary to be the kind of
servants they would need." Stephanie E. Jones-Rogers, *They Were Her Property: White Women
as Slave Owners in the American South* (New Haven: Yale University Press, 2019), xv, 15–16.

also spent more time than any of his siblings traveling with his father to manage the family's plantations. Bob Scott, John Addison's body servant, was their constant companion on these journeys. These trips contributed to Howell's lifelong affection for Bob and left him feeling "more attached to him than any negro, I know."[6] Difficulty reconciling this attachment with observations of the harsher realities experienced by others held in bondage likely encouraged Howell's determination never to be an active plantation manager. He began turning his eye instead toward a political career that allowed him to profit from and defend the South's peculiar institution. When he entered the University of Georgia as a teenager, he received a steady flow of encouragement from his parents and relatives to prepare himself for a career in public service. College life, however, devolved into a years-long escapade, fueled by "gin & water with a little sugar," that, in the words of a close friend and classmate, left few local prostitutes "un-Cobbed."[7] Nevertheless, he possessed the ambition and intelligence to focus when necessary and graduated fourth in his class. Following college, he rejected the opportunity to manage a family plantation and launched himself toward training in law. He steadfastly believed the daily management of the people his family enslaved was best left to someone else.

John B. Lamar ultimately became that someone. In early 1834 he had unsuccessfully courted Howell's younger sister, Laura. That relationship failed, but despite his disappointment John B. encouraged the courtship of Mary Ann and Howell later that year. The young couple wed in Athens in May 1835, following Howell's graduation and Zachariah's death. The new brothers-in-law, each barely twenty years old, saw the marriage as the genesis of a political dynasty. Together they formulated plans for how to rise to national office and marveled at the endless possibilities that their family names and wealth made possible.[8] Mary Ann encouraged these as-

---

6. Howell Cobb to Mary Ann Cobb, December 13, 1850.

7. Henry L. Benning to Howell Cobb, September 5, 1834; December 9, 1835.

8. Joseph P. Reidy argues that the sons of many plantation families declined to engage in politics at the national level because long absences in Washington, D.C., required long absences from home that interfered with the demands of administering their family estates. He notes that Howell avoided this limitation on his ambitions because of John B.'s willingness to undertake the supervision of all the Cobb-Lamar properties. Joseph P. Reidy, *From Slavery to Agrarian Capitalism in the Cotton Plantation South: Central Georgia, 1800–1880* (Chapel Hill: University of North Carolina Press, 1992), 52–53. For a similar marriage between a daughter of exceptional wealth and young man with political ambitions, as well as the need for her to manage their plantation holdings and enslaved laborers to allow for his rise in national politics, see Melanie Pavich-Lindsay, *Anna: The Letters of a St. Simons Plantation Mistress* (Athens:

pirations, writing to Howell that she would steer him toward his destiny as "not only a *good husband* but a great man."[9] The newlyweds began construction of a palatial home worthy of these dreams on land adjacent to John Addison and Sarah Cobb in Athens.

Both Howell and John B. scored early political victories in 1837. John B., who had taken up residence on the family's Swift Creek Plantation, won a seat representing Bibb County in the state legislature. Howell secured an appointment as solicitor general of the Western Judicial Circuit. Yet even as the walls of Mary Ann and Howell's new home went up, the foundations of the Cobb family's wealth began to collapse in the wake of that year's national financial panic. The economic downturn caught John Addison badly overextended and forced him into bankruptcy. Worse still, Howell had cosigned most of his father's loans and was also pulled down by the disaster. John B. unwittingly complicated Howell and Mary Ann's problems by grossly exceeding their budget when dispatched to New York to purchase furniture for their new home. Ruin followed as a flurry of court-ordered sales liquidated virtually the entire Cobb fortune. Yet Mary Ann's enormous wealth remained intact. In a rare assertion of a woman's ability to maintain legal rights to own property, the trustees appointed in her father's will had required the couple to sign a premarital contract. Mary Ann's assets thereafter remained legally separate from those of her husband.[10]

The foresight of the trustees and Mary Ann's money allowed Howell to

University of Georgia Press, 2002), xxi–xxiv. For John B.'s wealth and his willingness to take on this role on behalf of his sister and brother-in-law, see Richard W. Iobst, *Civil War Macon* (Macon: Mercer University Press, 2009), 9.

9. Mary Ann Cobb to Howell Cobb, April 1836.

10. Under early nineteenth-century common law, a woman's property became her husband's upon marriage, and she could become liable for his debts after his death. Woody Holton argues that in the wake of the Panic of 1837, states began to pass equity laws that enabled women to protect their assets through legal agreements. Prenuptial contracts proved rare even after 1837, but they were exceedingly so when Mary Ann and Howell were married in 1835. Woody Holton, "Equality as Unintended Consequence: The Contracts Clause and the Married Women's Property Acts," *Journal of Southern History* 81, no. 2 (May 2015): 313–40. See also Jones-Rogers, *They Were Her Property*, 31–37, 61–70; Marie S. Molloy, *Single, White, Slaveholding Women in the Nineteenth-Century American South* (Columbia: University of South Carolina Press, 2018), 17–18, 140, 162–63; James C. Cobb, "What Kind of Cobb Are You? Class, Wealth, and Power in the Real and Remembered South," *Southern Cultures* 22, no. 4 (Winter 2016): 114–18; Pavich-Lindsay, *Anna*, xxi–xxii; George C. Rable, *Civil Wars: Women and the Crisis of Nationalism* (Urbana: University of Illinois, 1991), 22–24; Norma Basch, "Equity vs. Equality: Emerging Concepts of Women's Political Status in the Age of Jackson," *Journal of the Early Republic* 3, no. 3 (Autumn 1983): 297–318; Catherine Clinton, *The Plantation Mistress: Woman's World in the Old South* (Chapel Hill: University of North Car-

continue his political ambitions, even as his parents struggled to rebuild their lives. He and John B. were both still so young, and John B. and Mary Ann so wealthy, that they viewed Howell's bankruptcy as a temporary financial setback rather than a career-ending event. Their aspirations undiminished, both men ran for, and were elected to, the U.S. Congress in 1842. This grand success left them facing an unexpected quandary over how to move to Washington, D.C., while simultaneously managing their assets. John B. recognized that the entire family's fortunes now depended on the profitability of their plantations. He also knew that Howell was wholly unprepared to provide the management necessary to attain that goal. He graciously stepped away from the elected office he had long sought, writing his beloved brother-in-law, "I shall never be able to acquire that prominence to which you are destined."[11] John B. would stay behind, run the family's empire, provide for his sister and her children, and use their position to propel Howell to the highest reaches of government, promising him "to aid in sustaining you in your career hereafter."[12] Howell, Mary Ann, and John B. had always been exceptionally close. John B.'s decision, however, inextricably wove together the emotional, financial, and political interests of the three.

For his part, John B. kept his promise to carefully manage the family's holdings so their wealth could sustain Howell's meteoric rise. Zachariah's 1834 will gifted his children agricultural land in ten Georgia counties as well as additional lands in Alabama. Howell had been positioned to inherit Cherry Hill Plantation, but his father's subsequent bankruptcy left the future of the plantation in doubt until John B. quietly purchased it and secured its position within the family's holdings. By the mid-1840s, the network of family plantations included properties in Walton County (Cowpens Plantation), Baldwin County (Hurricane, Harris Place, and Cedar Shoals Plantations), Bibb County (Swift Creek Plantation), and Jefferson County (Cherry Hill Plantation). Within a matter of years, John B. had shifted the focus of this partnership with his sister and brother-in-law southward into Sumter County (Bivins, Butts, Dominy, Jackson Place, Scrutchins, and Spring Creek Plantations) and Worth County (Worth Place Plantation), while retaining ownership of the Baldwin and Bibb County plantations.

olina Press, 1982), 34–35; and Bertram Wyatt-Brown, *Southern Honor: Ethics and Behavior in the Old South* (Oxford: Oxford University Press, 1982), 255–58.

11. John B. Lamar to Howell Cobb, October 26, 1842.
12. Ibid.

At its farthest reaches, this span of plantations covered nearly two hundred miles in Georgia, as well as additional plantations in Alabama and Florida.[13] Even if the Cobb-Lamars had desired to live part of the year on their agricultural holdings, as did most other elite planter families, the sheer number of plantations as well as the great distance between them made such arrangements all but impossible. This was not accidental. The amount of land and enslaved people that Zachariah's children inherited taught them that, in such an economy of scale, they could afford to manage it differently than did many of their peers. Moreover, none of them found plantation life congenial. They built their empire in a way that allowed them to stay in their in-town residences, where they preferred to be. They created a proto-corporate model to manage their expansive holdings instead of embracing the traditional roles of planters. They recognized that their constant presence on the plantations mattered less than their capacity to hire effective overseers to serve as the daily managers of their dispersed empire.

Administering the more than twenty thousand acres and hundreds of human beings his family owned led John B. to employ a style of management that was more scientific and corporate in its design than was practiced by many of his less-affluent peers. He, like some few other absentee owners of large-scale plantations, found it highly profitable to embrace a form of organization that foreshadowed the scientific management systems advocated by late-nineteenth-century industrialists.[14] John B.'s or-

13. John B. felt the Alabama and Florida plantations were too far removed from their other operations to be administered efficiently. He sold the Florida plantation in 1846 and the Alabama plantation following the death of his and Mary Ann's brother, Andrew, in 1848.

14. In her study of absentee owners of large Caribbean and southern plantations, historian Caitlin Rosenthal provocatively argues that this method of management was highly profitable. Rosenthal attributes this profitability to its reliance on what the Nobel Prize–winning economist Oliver Williamson later called the "M-form, or multidivisional form, because it combined the strategic functions of a central office with the operating efficiency of smaller divisions." The unimpeded flow of information through this structure, she argues, "offered the potential for sophisticated coordination of operations on a remarkable scale." Caitlin Rosenthal, *Accounting for Slavery: Masters and Management* (Cambridge: Harvard University Press, 2018), 17–31, 41–48. See also Alan L. Olmstead and Paul W. Rhode, "Cotton, Slavery, and the New History of Capitalism," *Explorations in Economic History* 67 (2018): 1–17; Caitlin Rosenthal, "Slavery's Scientific Management: Masters and Managers," in Sven Beckert and Seth Rockman, eds., *Slavery's Capitalism: A New History of American Economic Development* (Philadelphia: University of Pennsylvania Press, 2016), 66–74; Edward Baptist, "Toward a Political Economy of Slave Labor: Hands, Whipping Machines, and Modern Power," in *Slavery's Capitalism: A New History of American Economic Development*, ed. Sven Beckert and Seth Rockman (Philadelphia: University of Pennsylvania Press, 2016), 31–33; Adam Rothman, *Slave Country: American Expansion and the Origins of the Deep South* (Cambridge: Harvard Uni-

ganizational model created a network of vertically integrated plantations that ran on the free flow of massive amounts of written information and through the endless physical movement of resources and people between the family's holdings. Each of the family's plantations was both a self-sufficient enterprise and part of an interconnected network along which they transferred workers, food, tools, and livestock from one site to another.

Overseers provided the critical link in making this arrangement function. John B. sought out individuals who could manage each of the family's holdings with an awareness of the complexities of their roles. He attempted to hire only married men of "good conduct" who could compel the enslaved workforce to be productive without being brutal and provoking open resistance. A good overseer, he believed, had to simultaneously produce profits from cash crops and raise sufficient pork and corn so as to avoid the purchase of outside provisions for the sustenance of the enslaved, and to do both without demanding too much work or engaging in excessive punishments.[15] He also expected his overseers to understand their responsibility for maintaining an essential branch within the larger system he administered. Failure to produce enough materials or food, or to maintain the health and compliance of the enslaved, jeopardized the individual plantation as well as its role in the broader network.

In addition to overseers' responsibility for managing the daily minutiae of plantation production, John B. also required them to provide regular written reports accounting for progress and hindrances in fulfilling their duties. He, in turn, relayed critical information to his sister and brother-in-law and made decisions about moving people and supplies between sites. This arrangement proved highly beneficial, yet it placed an enormous burden on John B.'s shoulders.

By the mid-1840s, his frustration with the constant dismissal and hiring of overseers compelled him to write Howell and Mary Ann that the three of them should consider selling everything and simply reinvesting the proceeds in U.S. government bonds.[16] Ultimately, he determined it best to adhere to that which he already knew, rather than risking their

---

versity Press, 2005), 223, 177–78, 189; Reidy, *From Slavery to Agrarian Capitalism*, 5–9, 82–86; and Mart Stewart, *"What Nature Suffers to Groe": Life, Labor, and Landscape on the Georgia Coast, 1680–1920* (Athens: University of Georgia Press, 1996), 112–13.

15. John B. Lamar to Howell Cobb, January 5, 1846; John B. Lamar, overseer contract with John Roberson, November 4, 1846.

16. John B. Lamar to Howell Cobb, May 23, 1846.

fortune on the uncertainty of financial markets. His decision brought the family incredible wealth. He purchased one of the largest and most opulent houses in Macon, which he named the Bear's Den. His affluence made him one of Macon's most eligible bachelors, but he never married. Income from the plantations funded his frequent tours of northern and European cities. It allowed him time to author a series of short stories, published anonymously in various newspapers and magazines in the 1840s and 1850s.[17] He also devoted extensive time to serving as a surrogate father for Howell and Mary Ann's children during Howell's long absences in Washington, D.C. He spent extensive periods with his nephews and nieces when they stayed with him in his Macon home. He also aided in the selection of schools for the boys' educations and introduced them to the complexities of plantation management, just as Zachariah and John Addison had done for him and Howell. Most importantly, he remained Howell's closest friend and advisor and Mary Ann's constant support.

With Mary Ann and John B. as his partners, Howell pushed his raw talent and the family's extensive resources into a brilliant political career. He was elected to Congress five times and ultimately rose to become Speaker of the House of Representatives from 1849 to 1851. Speaker Cobb guided the House to support the Compromise of 1850 and secured Georgia's acceptance of it. He was elected governor of Georgia in late 1851, then reelected to Congress in 1855. Although he declined efforts to return him to the speakership, he accepted the post of secretary of the treasury in the Buchanan administration in 1857. Secretary Cobb steered the nation through the financial crisis of 1857, but the bitter struggle over "Bleeding Kansas" eroded his faith in political compromise and moved him to a more radical stance on the deteriorating sectional situation. He unsuccessfully sought the Democratic nomination for the pres-

17. John B. Lamar's short stories initially appeared in the Milledgeville *Federal Union*, the *Ladies' Mirror*, the Macon *Telegraph*, and *Spirit of the Times*, and they were subsequently reprinted in the *Family Companion* as "Homespun Yarns" (1851). The historian Bernard DeVoto noted the broad reach of Lamar's literary influence, even if he subsequently has been left out of the American canon, claiming that his story "Polly Peablossom's Wedding" (1842) was a direct source for some of Mark Twain's writings. Bernard DeVoto, *Mark Twain's America* (1932; repr., Lincoln: University of Nebraska Press, 1997), 158. The scholar M. Thomas Inge claimed that Lamar's story "The 'Experience' of the Blacksmith in the Mountain Pass" was the source for Charles Dickens's tale, "Colonel Quagg's Conversion." M. Thomas Inge, ed., *The Frontier Humorists: Critical Views* (Hamden, Conn.: Shoestring Press, 1975), 8. See also Lawrence Huff, "The Lamar-Dickens Connection," *Mississippi Quarterly* 40, no. 2 (Spring 1987): 113–15.

idency in 1860, then resigned his cabinet post following Lincoln's election. After leading the Georgia secession effort, he became president of the Provisional Congress of the Confederate States of America. In 1861, having been passed over for the presidency of the CSA, he swore in Jefferson Davis to that office.[18]

Although Mary Ann began her marriage promising to help Howell become all he might be, his success came at the cost of seldom being available to her as a "good husband." She gave birth to twelve children, six of whom died in childhood. She often experienced the joy of their births and grief over their deaths alone, as Howell's career kept him largely away from home for more than two decades. Although she sometimes joined him in Washington, D.C., or in Milledgeville during his governorship, she refused to make either city her home. John B. assisted her when he could, but she also relied heavily on an enslaved woman named Aggy Carter to help raise her children. Aggy was, in turn, one of a large group of household laborers. Mary Ann single-handedly managed their work and daily lives while remaining keenly aware of their connections within the larger network of those enslaved by the family. She did all this while also functioning as an equal partner to her husband and brother in debating politics and plantation management.[19]

She was an astute political advisor and confidante who aided her husband in becoming "a great man." She guided him through the potential hazards of the political arena as he climbed from local office to the presidential cabinet. Once he arrived at the center of the national political stage, she flawlessly fulfilled the gracious role her father had raised her to play. After decades of hosting large events in her private homes and the governor's mansion, she was more than qualified to carry the role into the White House. The president and his secretary of the trea-

18. For Howell's political career, see Randy L. Reid, "Howell Cobb of Georgia: A Biography," PhD diss., Louisiana State University, 1995.

19. Little has been written about elite women who, like Mary Ann, assumed the role of full and equal business partner in the management of plantations. The most compelling recent scholarship on elite women's power over the lives of the enslaved comes from Stephanie E. Jones-Rogers, who argues that these women often used their positions within the household to protect their property for the future security of their children, even when it meant challenging the authority of their husbands or holding tight rein on the actions of overseers. Jones-Rogers, *They Were Her Property*, 27–32, 63–70. See also Cynthia Kennedy, *Braided Relations, Entwined Lives: The Women of Charleston's Urban Slave Society* (Bloomington: Indiana University Press, 2005), 77–94; Elizabeth Fox-Genovese, *Within the Plantation Household: Black and White Women of the Old Plantation South* (Chapel Hill: University of North Carolina Press, 1988), 97, 205–6; and Clinton, *Plantation Mistress*, 30–33.

sury had been close friends for years, so much so that Buchanan insisted Howell live with him in the White House for months before Mary Ann's arrival in Washington, D.C.[20] Once she was there, the bachelor president relied on her and his niece, Harriet Lane, to join him in hosting formal events. When the Prince of Wales visited the White House in October 1860, Mary Ann sat at the president's side during the state dinner but missed her chance to dance with the future King Edward VII when the president forbade dancing at the event.[21] Howell hosted the president and the prince on a visit to Washington's tomb at Mount Vernon two days later. An image of the solemn occasion appeared on the cover of the next issue of *Harper's Weekly* and was then commemorated in a large painting by Thomas Rossiter that now hangs in the Smithsonian Institution.

Howell, Mary Ann, and John B. lived remarkable, gilded lives. Yet the wealth and freedom to fulfill their dreams was made possible only by the freedom they stole from the hundreds of people they enslaved.

The people they kept enslaved lived and worked daily before their eyes but were never fully seen. The family recorded incidents in the lives of the enslaved almost as afterthoughts in thousands of letters. Looked at individually, these fleeting moments appear incredibly prosaic. Among the countless scraps of information lost in larger narratives about the white family is news, for example, that Sylvia received word through Mary Ann of her daughters on the plantation, or that John B. had sent Berry to learn to cook in the kitchen of his cousin in Americus, or that Howell consented to Aggy marrying Isaac. Yet piecing together tiny fragments, rather than viewing only a few documents at a time, opens up a slightly broader view of the lives of the enslaved. It also reveals that they existed within a remarkable and complicated series of interconnections between the plantations and the townhomes in Athens and Macon.

The Cobb-Lamar family undoubtedly excelled at constructing a social and political network that propelled them to national prominence.[22] Un-

---

20. Howell Cobb to Mary Ann Cobb, May 13, 1859; Howell Cobb to Mary Ann Cobb, September 16, 1859; Kate Thompson to Mary Ann Cobb, May 18, 1859; Howell Cobb to Mary Ann Cobb, May 9, 1859, Cobb-Erwin-Lamar Family Collection, Hargrett Rare Book and Manuscript Library, University of Georgia, Athens; *Greenville Patriot Mountaineer*, cited in *Southern Banner* (Athens), March 26, 1857.

21. Mary Ann Cobb to Lamar Cobb, October 13, 1860, Cobb-Erwin-Lamar Family Collection.

22. The importance of mapping the dense network the Cobb-Lamars created and used to such great advantage has been informed in large part by the work of historian Niall Ferguson, among others. In a grand argument spanning several centuries of evidence, Ferguson argues that historians have long focused on vertical networks, which, by their very nature,

dergirding this visible connection between poles of influence was a less easily seen but equally dense set of pathways that passed material goods, financial and intellectual capital, and people back and forth among their properties. Everything they built aboveground grew out of the perfectly functioning root system that worked tirelessly below it. There is perhaps nothing surprising in identifying the complex infrastructure that sustained a wealthy, white family. It is rarer, however, to be able to see it transposed down.

None of the people in this book existed outside the family's network or the one the enslaved made within it. More to the point, the enslaved used the same web of connectivity to invisibly build and preserve their own world.[23] Enslaved couriers like Bob Scott and George Carter were

---

leave behind extensive paper trails documenting both decision by those in power and the ways in which they have been carried out by those below. He contends, however, that real creativity occurs along the less formal, less hierarchical, and therefore less documented horizontal networks that exist among families, peers, and coworkers. Niall Ferguson, *The Square and the Tower: Networks and Power, from the Freemasons to Facebook* (New York: Penguin Press, 2018), 17–18, 23–29, 46–48. Ferguson's discussion of network theory and "betweenness centrality," or the mapping of the individuals with the most important connections, is a profound analysis of the types of dense social networks examined by scholars of the antebellum South over the past several decades. For representative works in the field, see Adam L. Tate, *Conservatism and Southern Intellectuals, 1789–1861: Liberty, Tradition, and the Good Society* (Columbia: University of Missouri Press, 2005); Michael O'Brien, *Conjectures of Order: Intellectual Life and the American South, 1810–1860* (Chapel Hill: University of North Carolina Press, 2004); Michael O'Brien, ed., *All Clever Men, Who Make Their Way: Critical Discourse in the Old South* (Athens: University of Georgia Press, 1992); and especially Drew Gilpin Faust, *A Sacred Circle: The Dilemma of the Intellectual in the Old South, 1840–1860* (Baltimore: Johns Hopkins University Press, 1977).

23. Numerous scholars have acknowledged that the enslaved maintained ties of kinship and affection across plantation lines or beyond their masters' lots in town. Most significantly, Anthony Kaye's examination of pension applications from former Union soldiers revealed "neighborhoods" of plantations in which the enslaved from adjoining plantations communicated, married, and built kinship networks across formal plantation boundaries. Anthony E. Kaye, *Joining Places: Slave Neighborhoods of the Old South* (Chapel Hill: University of North Carolina Press, 2007). See also Tim Lockley, "The Forming and Fracturing of Families on a South Carolina Rice Plantation, 1812–1865," *History of the Family* 23, no. 1 (March 2018): 78–80; Emily West, *Chains of Love: Slave Couples in Antebellum South Carolina* (Urbana: University of Illinois Press, 2004), 27, 44, 52–54; Dylan C. Penningroth, *The Claims of Kinfolk: African American Property and Community in the Nineteenth-Century South* (Chapel Hill: University of North Carolina Press, 2003), 80–82, 85–88; Lorena S. Walsh, *From Calabar to Carter's Grove: The History of a Virginia Slave Community* (Charlottesville: University of Virginia Press, 1997), 1–21, 171–203, 220–26; Peter Kolchin, *American Slavery, 1619–1877* (New York: Hill and Wang, 1993), 148–49, 151–54; Ann Patton Malone, *Sweet Chariot: Slave Family and Household Structure in Nineteenth-Century Louisiana* (Chapel Hill: University of North Carolina Press, 1992), 1–3, 65–68, 76–115, 251–54; Orville Vernon Burton, *In My Father's House Are Many Mansions: Family and Community in Edgefield, South Carolina* (Chapel Hill: University of North

fundamental in facilitating this process as they traveled frequently among the family's plantations.[24] They knew, and were known to, all of the people at each location. They transported material goods such as carriages, clothes, lumber, boxes of supplies, butter, hams, and molasses. More poignantly, they conveyed other enslaved people as they were called up to the white households or sent back to labor on the plantations. Most importantly, in carrying news between and about members of the Cobb-Lamar family, they also kept the enslaved community connected to one another through shared messages about sickness and health, pregnancies, births, and deaths. The majority of people owned by the family were not isolated and disconnected but part of a vast and complex ecosystem of relationships and information that flowed back and forth.

Mary Ann, Howell, and John B. failed to appreciate the extent to which the network that sustained them also provided an essential asset to those who were enslaved. They never fully grappled with the effects of the invisible world being perpetually constructed just below their gazes. They did not discern the extent to which the people they kept enslaved spent lifetimes developing small ways of manipulating the system to make their own lives better. They did not see that the enslaved not only understood their own positions in the network but also frequently acted or reacted based on where they understood themselves to be and wanted to go. They refused to acknowledge the depth of the emotional lives, dreams, desires, and ambitions of the human beings they owned.

Carolina Press, 1985), 151–52, 163–64, 168–71; and Charles Joiner, *Down by the Riverside: A South Carolina Slave Community* (Urbana: University of Illinois Press, 1984, 132–33. While those enslaved by the Cobb-Lamars resided within similar geographically bound communities and connected with enslaved people on adjoining plantations, they were also aware of their places in a larger community defined by the multi-plantation network that spanned the state.

24. It is worth noting that Bob and George, like a large percentage of other enslaved people in this book, had surnames. There is no way of knowing how many of the total number of people owned by the Cobb-Lamars had, or used, last names. For those who did, however, there is no record of how they came upon their names. Herbert Gutman suggests that many enslaved people used former owners' surnames, perhaps more frequently than antebellum legal records indicate, as a way of demarcating family lines. Herbert Gutman, *The Black Family in Slavery and Freedom, 1750–1925* (New York: Vintage Books, 1976), 236–50. See also Kaye, *Joining Places,* 64; Malone, *Sweet Chariot,* 239; John C. Inscoe, "Generation and Gender as Reflected in Carolina Slave Naming Practices," *South Carolina Historical Magazine* 94, no. 4 (October 1993): 262; Kolchin, *American Slavery,* 140; Cheryll Ann Cody, "There Was No 'Absalom' on the Ball Plantations: Slave-Naming Practices in the South Carolina Low Country, 1720–1865," *American Historical Review* 92, no. 3 (June 1987); Burton, *In My Father's House Are Many Mansions,* 164–65; and Joiner, *Down by the Riverside,* 221–22.

For all she was blind to in her own world, Mary Ann recognized the future lurking just beyond the horizon. She counseled her children to preserve the mountains of correspondence, about matters large and small, professional and personal, that had kept the family empire functioning for years. "File [it] away," she told them, as "it will be *historical* when I am dead."[25] Yet neither she nor her husband nor her brother saw any historic value in the lives of those they enslaved. In countless throwaway lines on the fringes of those letters are traces of the lives of the people they owned, people who were before their eyes daily but who they never fully saw.

Last Will and Testament of Zachariah Lamar

Milledgeville, January 23, 1832

In the name of God Amen, I Zachariah Lamar . . . being of sound and disposing mind and memory, do make, ordain, publish, and declare, this to be my last will and testament, revoking all others. . . .[26]

I give bequeath and demise unto . . . my beloved son John Bassil Lamar, the real and personal property in this clause hereinafter to be mentioned. . . all my plantation and real estate in Bibb County. . . [and] Twiggs County, containing . . . five thousand one hundred and sixty two acres. Also the negroes hereinafter mentioned to wit; Old Charles, Liny, Milind, Clarisa, Joshua, Mincaly, Randal, Julia Ann, Young Charles, Selah, Walker, Phil & Phoeba his wife, Philip, Lucinda, John (son of Phil), Augustus, Gabriel, Mary & her child Leacy, Ned, Sam Herbert, Nancy his wife, Caswell, Sarah Ann child of Sam Herbert, Abram, Blacksmith, Clarisa his wife, Louisa, Jane, Scipio, Sarah, Mathew, Scipio (son of Old Scipio) Sarah Scipios child, Isaiah, Billy Bird, Grace, Lucy, Billy son of Billy Bird, Caty (daughter of Billy Bird) Antonette John (son of Billy

---

25. Mary Ann Cobb to Lamar Cobb, October 13, 1860, Cobb-Erwin-Lamar Family Collection.

26. Zachariah appointed his kinsmen L. Q. C. Lamar and Jesse Robinson to serve as trustees for all three of his children. L. Q. C. Lamar was the son of Zachariah's brother, John, and the father of future senator and U.S. Supreme Court justice L. Q. C. Lamar II. Jesse Robinson was Zachariah's brother-in-law and a prominent planter. Mary Ann resided in Robinson's home when she first moved to Athens following her father's death.

Bird) Matt, Venus, Mark, Phillis, Joe & (Luan his wife) Robbin, Polly, Armstrong, George, Francis, Elijah, Ned (Carpenter) African Peter, (Fanny his wife), Paul, Simon, Andrew, Hamilton, Peter, & Harit his sister, Edinborough, Sally, Cecilia, Adalaide, Beck, child of big Flora, Maria, Esau, Viney, daughter of Scipio and all the future increase of all of the negroes aforesaid. . . .

I give and bequeath . . . [to] my beloved daughter, Mary Ann Lamar . . . [my] Lands in the county of Baldwin containing twenty four hundred and thirty six acres; also the following negroes, to wit. Levin, Nancy, (his wife), Nelly, Elizabeth, Dilia (children of Levin,) Elick and Clarisa (his wife) and James, (their child) Ben, Robinson, & (Patsy his) wife, and their five children to wit Rhoda, Fleming, Henrietta, Ann, [Alsey?], Jeffrey, Rhina and her two children, Shadrack, and Ellick, Sam son of Levin, Abram, and Hetty, his wife and their child Milkey, Joe, Blacksmith, and Lucy, his wife, October and Sylvia, his wife, and their five children to wit Vicey, Jane, Sam, Elbert, & Daniel; May and Easter [his] wife and their four children to wit, Maria, Izrael, Betsey, & Pleasant, Edmund & Creasy his wife and their three children, to wit, Ambrose, Minty, & Scott; Simon and his wife Peggy and their two children to wit. Martha & Phoebe; Isaac & Harriet his wife, and their child Wilson, Damon & Sibby his wife and their two children, Carolin & Isabella, Peggy & her two children, to wit Serena & Chaney, Levi, Ben Brewer, Rachael & Becky, her sister Crena and her brother Andrew, Moses, Sukey, Jim, Willis, Julyann, & Rosanna, their sister Sukey, & Amy her sister, Janey, Lewis & his brother Joe; And the future increase of the female negroes aforesaid. . . .

I give bequeath and demise unto my beloved son Andrew Jackson Lamar . . . all my Land in Bibb County . . . containing one Thousand two hundred & twenty two acres; also Lots [totaling 1,169 acres in] Early County; also . . . twenty two hundred acres of Land . . . in now Lownds County, formerly Montgomery County in the State of Alabama; also the following negroes to wit. Young Mark, Young Frank, Caty daughter of Hercules, Mary (Big Floras child), Baker, & Selina; and the future increase of the said female negroes; also one hundred shares of State Bank Stock now held by me, also fourteen thousand Dollars . . . it is my will and desire that my son Andrew Jackson Lamar shall receive a liberal education at any eligible institution in the State of Georgia. . . .

It is my will and desire that the residue of my Lands in Alabama, not demised, shall also be sold by my Executors according to Law and the proceeds divided among children.

Codicil to the Last Will and Testament
of Zachariah Lamar
Milledgeville, May 22, 1832

In the name of God Amen.

I Zachariah Lamar . . . do by this codicil, to my last will & testament . . . [bequeath to] my beloved son John Bassil Lamar; the following negroes, additional to his legacy, in my last will & testament, above mentioned, to wit, Jim Darby, his wife Chana & their children, Malind, & Chiny, Boson, Nancy his wife & their children Mary Ann & an infant; Hercules, Flora, his wife, & their child Landon, Jim, Nancy, & their future increase.

And I do also give . . . unto my said son John B. Lamar . . . [391 acres in] Twiggs County, also . . . [1,430 acres in] Wilkinson County. . . also [202 acres in] . . . Laurens County. . . . Also one House & Lot in the Town of Milledgeville situate on Wayne street. . . .

I give . . . [to] my beloved daughter Mary Ann Lamar, the following negroes additional to her legacy in my last will and testament aforesaid, to wit Frank, Charity, his wife; Mingo, Mary his wife & their children Cybella, and Rosetta, Cyrus, Sukey his wife & their children Emanuel & Anderson, Jenny, & her child Solomon, and Dennis & their future increase . . . I do also give [her]. . . All such Lands lying and being in the Counties of Houston, Dooly, Irwin & Early not heretofore bequeathed or demised, of which I may be possessed at the time of my death . . . [and three lots] and all the buildings thereon, all lying and being in the town of Milledgeville.

I will . . . unto my beloved son Andrew Jackson Lamar, the following negroes Additional to his legacy, in my last will and testament aforesaid viz, Susan child of old Jenny, Mingo son of Old Mingo, Keziah daughter of August, Jane daughter of Mingo, Henry, & Ghent, children of Cyrus; also an additional sum of two thousand Dollars; also fifteen hundred and fifty seven acres of Land . . . in Baldwin County . . . [and 202 acres in] Houston County.

Mary Ann Cobb to Howell Cobb

Athens, November 16, 1836

Uncle [Jesse] Robinson went from home and left no winter clothes for Susan, although he expects to remain until Christmas. Rachael tells me that Susan had some woollen clothes but did not bring them with her to Athens.

I wish you would tell her mammy to send them up to her.

John B. Lamar to Howell Cobb

Macon, August 16, 1837

An overseer with a small family is most desirable. A single man is objectionable on many accounts, he will have few ties to bind him at home, & is disposed to be absent too much & moreover he causes disturbances among the negroes, by interfering with their domestic arrangements. A married man will be home at night with his family & has fewer inducements to call him off. . . .

A married man has given good security for his behavior in his wife & children, a single man can give no pledge, he acts well as long as it suits *him* & plays the devil when he chooses, thinking that no person that he cares for will be affected by it.

I would trust a man of family much sooner in any situation than a single man.

This is preaching up principles that I do not follow myself—you will laugh & say. Well.

Sarah Rootes Cobb to Mary Ann Cobb

Augusta, December 21, 1837

Phillis keeps quite well so do all the others, and all send their remembrances to their relations.

Riny J. Lamar[27] to Seiny

Milledgeville, June 29, 1839

My Dear Mother

I write to inform you that I lost my baby last Tuesday was a week a go. All of the family are very well. If you can possible do so you must let me hear from you all soon. Give my love to all and except the same.

Your affectionate daughter.

Riny Lamar
to Seiny

D. Dickson to John B. Lamar

Covington, September 21, 1839

My overseer has kept a close watch for Jim but has not seen any thing of him. I have not heard from him since he saw you at the Camp Ground. I was in hopes he would come in to get his wages, but I now fear he will not. I am Inclined to think he is yet in the nabourhood as he has taken up with a negro woman at my plantation. I will make every exhirtions to get him & secure him.

Joseph McGhee[28] to John B. Lamar

Swift Creek Plantation, September 22, 1839

I have nothing worth of your attention to rite you at this time. The Family is all well but Leucy little pompey & Francis has taken sick a gain. She is note very sick. . . . I have caught Jim darby & has pute him in jail. I

---

27. Riny J. Lamar is noted as "Rhina" in Zachariah Lamar's will and was enslaved on the Hurricane Plantation. It is possible that she was one of the seventy-four descendants of Charles and Seny Walker, who were enslaved at Swift Creek Plantation. Riny directed her letter to John B. Lamar in Macon, which lay just across the Ocmulgee River from Swift Creek. Charles and Seny appear to have been at the Bears Den with some frequency, and there are indications that Lamar shared news about his and their families with them.

28. An overseer at Swift Creek Plantation.

caught him on Saturday night . . . he has got a free pas. John Humphreys of Paulding County is sine to it.

Robert Habersham to Howell Cobb
Savannah, June 16, 1840

I have received yours of the 7th inst. and in reply would remark that under the circumstances, I must ask that a new mortgage should be executed on the negroes, mortgaged to me before, for the security of the note originally given by your Father to me. . . .

Copy of note . . . for which the assigned ninety negroes are mortgaged. $5256.55

Savannah 28th of April, 1832
On the first day of January next I promise to pay to Rob. Habersham Esq or order, at either of the Banks in Savannah Five thousand two hundred & fifty six 55/100 dollars, for value received.
Signed, J. A. Cobb

Interest paid in land note to 15 June, and or about of principal $735.17.

Names of negroes mortgaged to secure—the payment of note to R. Habersham for $5256.55 as described. . . .

Ben, Eady, Anderson, Jim, Jane, Franses, Dolly, Leah, Nancy, Neptune, Ben, Young Eady, Nelly, Henry, Davy, Mary, Lavinia, Jeffrey, Bullah, Reuben, Sandy, Delila, Lucy, Peggy, Polly, Nancy, Abram, Jack, Soloman, Meshack, Lavinia & Infant, Mary, Betty, Little Meshack, Christian, Tinay, Suky, Charity, Mitchell, Richard, George, Eliza, Garten, Little George, Silvy, Jack, Phil, Willis, Patsy, George, Aheas, Lucy, Davy, Jesse, Tempy, Susan, Judy, Lethy, Lucy, Gabe, Turner, Caroline & Infant, Milly, Sally, Polly, Robert, William, Little Eda, Harriet, Mary, Wm, Richard, William, Maria & Infant, Polly, Flag, Benny, Martha, Sophy, Aggy, Little Gabe, Smith, Louisa & Infant, Bird, Robert, Young Ben.

David Gibson[29] to Howell Cobb

Hurricane Plantation, September 13, 1840

I have the women & children picking cotton & the men clearing & reparing. Several of the negroes sick, Mary esther Issabel vicy silvy of the women, Andrew & Ben Crowe of the men, Ezekiel risdel & anthony of the children. The two last named risdel & anthony Dangerous with the fever. Rinors child died last wednesday night. Stock generally in good order.

Joseph McGhee to John B. Lamar

Swift Creek Plantation, October 9, 1840

I have nothing new. It is very sickly in the settlement . . . al of the negros is sick non daingers at this time. Lewan baby is ded. It died with the bowel complainte. Francis has loste one. Leucy has loste one. She was taken sick two weaks before she loste hern. We have had a grate deal of sickness on the Plantation sence the two laste monts. There has bin 17 sick at one time with the chil an Fever. It is note so sickly now as it has bin. George has bin very low. He had the pleurisy bute he has gote well.

Mary Ann Cobb to John B. Lamar

Athens, February 8, 1841

The sale in Jefferson exceeded Howell's expectations. The negroes sold for ($26,300)—twenty six thousand & three hundred dollars.

Those in Watkinsville were not sold so well, but when the scarcity of money and this part of the county being a poor cotton growing country are taken into consideration, it is as good as could be expected. The amount they brought was 21,400$. Howell had hoped to sell the plantation corn, stock, tools, and negroes in a mass for $55,000 but was disappointed. . . .

---

29. An overseer at Hurricane Plantation.

If I could influence him he should never endorse another note as long as life lasts, for as this business shows it is not safe even between father & son.

William Livingston[30] to Howell Cobb
Cherry Hill Plantation, June 1, 1841

Bob got down on Saturday last with a letter stating that it was your request that Bob should bring as much corn as he could also the wool and butter. I have sent fore hundred and forty one pounds wool with sacks. . . . Tiby Betsey Patsey and [Love?] are laid up. Betsey is mending very fast and from fore to seven generally laid up. Teney runaway on 27th May. I have not herd from him since.

David Gibson to Howell Cobb
Hurricane Plantation, May 4, 1843

I [take] the present oppurtunity of writing you a few lines to inform you that your negroes are all well Except mingo Charity rinor Peggy and one of Hariets children. I would also state to you that I commenced howing my cotton last monday morning. I have worked the hands without a task and find that the hands will do near double what they did when they worked by tasks.[31] I have a verry good stand of cotton and have planted 300 & 9 acres of the best land on the plantation except one field. My corn crop is sorry for this time in the spring. I would be glad to see you soon, your stock are in good order. Several of the cattle died in the winter which make our milk & butter scarce during the spring & summer.

---

30. An overseer at Cherry Hill Plantation.

31. Under the task system, each enslaved laborer was required to meet a set limit of ground tended, or cotton picked, each day. After individuals completed their "task," they were generally allowed to use what remained of the day to provide for their own needs. Gibson's letter indicates the Cobb-Lamars were transitioning away from this model and toward one in which overseers supervised "gangs" of the enslaved who were worked from sunrise to sunset, usually with limited breaks.

W. I. & B. I. Hill to Howell Cobb
Monroe, July 10, 1843

Your kind favour by *boy Squire* is at hand and contents noted and we beg leave to say in reply that we have satisfied ourselves relative to his character and will give Mr. Newton a fair swap for him if he will trade for a young woman (say about twenty one or two) and a fine likely boy child some 3 months old.[32] The woman is as likely as one you will find in twenty under as good character as any girl. She is a good *cook washes* well *weaves* and *spins* and is a most excelent field hand. If Mr. Newton would like such a girl well enough to trade we will give him the girl and child and one hundred dollars payable next December for the boy and we are inclined to think it would be a very equitable trade. The boy we spoke of trading when you was over we have since declined doing so as we have a prospect of making sale of him and will suit us much better than the exchange then spoken of as our object is to turn him into money.

John B. Lamar to Mary Ann Cobb
Macon, September 5, 1843

Old Uncle Charles my aide de camp is now on a visit to his numerous posterity at the Hurricane, when he returns I can give you some account of things there. I have employed a man named Harvey for that place, next year.

Matthew Linam[33] to Howell Cobb
Cherry Hill Plantation, February 17, 1844

Silva children are well. Polly is verry smart to work. They appear to be satisfide with their granmother. I hear no complaint.

---

32. "Mr. Newton" probably refers to John Newton, a prominent Athens merchant and hotel owner. Hill and Hill appear to be brokering a deal to bring Squire to Walton County, where he could be closer to his wife Ellen at Cowpens Plantation.

33. An overseer at Cherry Hill Plantation.

Sarah Rootes Cobb to Mary Ann Cobb

Cowpens Plantation, March 6, 1844

How well [does] Sylvia do in her log cabin, after being used to a curtain bedstead. I expect it will go very hard with her, tell her we heard from her children. They were well, so is Jim. . . .

Gilbert (who had gained time and Williams had let him go to Athens) came and brought Howell's letter to John B. . . .

I told the children that night, that Mama had been to a ball, and they were perfectly astonished, as was Aggy who lifted up her hands in astonishment, you may tell [Howell] it caused a general laugh at his expence when we read of his visit to the barber's shop to curl his hair for him to appear at the presidents.

John B. Lamar to Mary Ann Cobb

Macon, May 20, 1844

If Congress is going to sit all summer hadn't I better go by the Cowpens & carry Aggy or Rachel on to you? If you desire it & Howell will write immediately, I shall get your letter in time, unless there is a failure in the mail.

I have just returned from the Hurricane & was at Cherry Hill about 8 days ago. The negroes are all well & sent, in their own language, "heap of howdeys to Master & Mistress." Since your departure & since they expect to see their master but seldom, they all seem to have taken a new impulse towards you both, more especially those at Cherry Hill.

Sarah Rootes Cobb to Mary Ann Cobb

Cowpens Plantation, June 9, 1844

I got sadly disappointed in getting a supply of butter from [Cherry Hill Plantation], Bob returned last night, and did not bring a single ounce for me . . . the overseer . . . sent the 50 wt of wool & 6 pounds of lambs wool for you and a ram & a ewe. . . . Bob says the crop is splendid and very clean. . . .

Polly and Eliza are both very hearty and the overseer writes Polly is a fine girl for work. They are very anxious to see their mother.

Sarah Rootes Cobb to Mary Ann Cobb
Cowpens Plantation, December 8, 1844

I shall try and send Bob over on tuesday, as the horses will have to carry our last load of cotton to the circle[34] tomorrow.

John B. Lamar to Howell Cobb
Macon, December 10, 1844

I have sent up 20 of the best hands from Cherry Hill to help pick out the Hurricane cotton and hope to do so by Christmas. We are behind hand in ginning in Baldwin in consequence of the gin & gear being worthless. I went to Clinton & bought a new gin & sent on Sunday. . . .

The negroes are all well at both places. Polly & Eliza are well & send their love to their mother.

John B. Lamar to Howell Cobb
Macon, February 7, 1845

The hands I sent up from [Cherry Hill Plantation] to pick out the Hurricane cotton, would I expect never have been sent home, unless I had gone & seen them off myself.

Lynam made a miserable crop of 105 bags of cotton, and a crop of corn that will not last more than half the year. In view of which in connection with the scarcity of meat there, as well as the demise of the three horses you bought for that place, which with a full force of hands, would render the purchase of several mules necessary, I concluded to curtail the force to 30 hands, and have sent the other 10 to the Hurricane where there is plenty of corn, more meat & more horse power, & where they can be more profitably employed.

---

34. Social Circle, Georgia.

Mary Ann Cobb to John B. Lamar

Washington, D.C., February 15, 1845

When you write, say how Howard is, and all you know about *Polly* and *Eliza* for Sylvias satisfaction, who is well and sends her love to Howard.

John B. Lamar to Mary Ann Cobb

Macon, February 22, 1845

Polly & Eliza are well. Howard is at Washington Hall, he has been sick, but has entirely recovered. I saw him a few days ago.

John B. Lamar to Mary Ann Cobb

Macon, May 11, 1845

Since I returned home, I have been to Jefferson & gave out clothes to the negroes, I found them all well, and the crop is doing well, but suffering some from drought. Polly & Eliza are well & send howdye to their mother. . . .

I shall go to the Hurricane on Thursday and give out the negroes their clothes there. . . .

I will endeavour to see about the purchase of the plantation adjoining the Hurricane, to move the Cherry hill negroes to, in the winter. Andrew is about to sell, and we must move somewhere, & I know of no place so convenient.

John B. Lamar to Mary Ann Cobb

Macon, December 2, 1845

In reading your letter, so full of details—I love details in a letter, they are so graphic & bring every thing so forcibly before me—I could realize pretty much what your sensations are in returning to a city, from the retirement of the country. The transition is so sudden from quiet to bustle, from the natural to the artificial in manners & customs. Your life for two years has been on the two extremes. Mine is so much the same way that I know just how it is. I am one half the year rattling over rough roads . . . stopping at farm houses in the country, scolding overseers in half a dozen counties & two states (Florida & Geo), and the other half in the largest cities of the Union, or those of Europe, living on dainties & riding on rail cars and steamboats.

Andrew Lamar to John B. Lamar
Columbus, December 12, 1845

Please say to the negroes I got from you as well as my own, that they will be sent for by the last of December to go to Jefferson. Say to Joe that he can take up his line of march for the Cowpens. . . .

In settling my place in Alabama, I have had to pick fifteen of my *best* hands and it weakened my force very much, particularly when it is taken into consideration the quantity of ground I have to keep under fence. And on that account if a division [of Florida slaves] can be effected, early in January I could carry my hands up to Jefferson and pitch my usual crop . . . however it will not make a *material* difference with me, if the negroes in Florida go on and make another crop provided we appoint some time in the spring to go down and divide, so that by Christmas 1846 I can send my slaves as a part of my second installment for Alabama.

I have left on my place 27 (twenty seven) hands with the six I have in Macon will make 33 hands I can work in Jefferson next year.

John B. Lamar to Mary Ann Cobb
Macon, January 23, 1846

I have the Cherry Hill people all moved up to the Harris place, which lies broadside with the Hurricane & with tolerable good land, has every necessary building for a plantation, except a sufficient number of negro houses, which I am having built. The business is now compact & will give me not one half the trouble it formerly has. I have turned off the Hurricane overseer for getting drunk, and have stirred up both the overseers to industry, which will last through one year I expect.

I have purchased . . . a plantation in Sumpter to remove some of my hands to, and if we have no war we can all make money.

John B. Lamar to Mary Ann Cobb

Macon, April 27, 1846

My man Ned the carpenter is idle or nearly so at the plantation. He is fixing gates & like the idle groom in Pickwick trying to fool himself into the belief that he is doing something. But on considering his general character for intemperance & disobedience & quarrelsomeness I have concluded it would be best to pay a little too much for the house, rather than inflict him on you at this time. While I was gone I had him in town & on returning found that he had been drunk & fighting and misbehaving in every way, so that I have banished him to rural life. He is an eye servant. If I was with him I could have the work done soon & cheap, but I am afraid to trust him off where there is no one he fears. He is doing literally nothing at home, and sparing him would not be a cents expense as to that, but I conclude that you do not feel like being annoyed, just now, as I fear & almost know he would annoy you, by getting drunk & raising a row on the lot. I shall sell the rascal the first chance I get.

John B. Lamar to Mary Ann Cobb

Macon, March 19, 1849

I came on by the Hurricane right to Swift Creek when I left your house. . . .

Old Aunt Seny was delighted with the basket you sent her. She & old Charles cherish & will cherish for the remainder of their lives, all the incidents of your visit at Swift Creek, almost like the Scotch peasantry do the summer visits of Victoria & her children. Old Charles said in his impressive manner, "I must think our mistress will come down & see us all again next winter. If she only *knowed* how proud it makes us all feel she would come again & stay longer."

Howell Cobb to Mary Ann Cobb

Milledgeville, November 12, 1849

A little incident occurred in the street yesterday that I know will amuse you. Benning & myself were walking along together when a little negro about fourteen years of age stepped up to us, & addressing Benning said "Howdye master," how are you says B, "how is *mistis* says the negro." I discovered then that it was one of our negroes & that he had mistaken Benning for me so I said, "I reckon it is me, you want to speak to." He looked around from Benning to me & with a broad grin on his face, he said, "*Why, yes, you are the very fellow.*" It gave us a hearty laugh & we passed on.

John B. Lamar to Mary Ann Cobb

Macon, February 18, 1850

The venerable worthies at Swift Creek, Old man Charles & Aunt Seny, have often hazarded the remark—as I have told you before I believe—that "Miss Mary Ann ought to have one 'gal,' she must want one." The old folks will no doubt be delighted to hear their wishes have become reality. They will be offended if I dont send an express out with the news—as they are the ancestors of 74 living descendants (who can be seen at Swift Creek, Sumpter & the Hurricane & Harris place by any person curious in such matters)—They as you may readily conceive, are very much interested in all that concerns the "increase and multiply" clause in the Bible.

John B. Lamar to Mary Ann Cobb

Philadelphia, April 25, 1850

We reached here today at 2½ o'clock. The boys have been perfectly delighted. I took them to the old state house & showed them the window from which the Declaration of Independence was first read. Also to the grave of Dr. Franklin & other interesting localities. But Tom Thumb at Barnums Museum was the object of the greatest attraction to them. There is a theatre attached to the museum & after tea Genl Thumb appeared on the stage in the costume of a Highland chief. . . . And between his exhibitions a dancing girl with very short skirts appeared & danced to the great astonishment of the boys, who had never seen such performances by the young ladies of Athens. . . . The show concluded by a play . . . in which there was a great deal of dancing & some fighting, and it being the first theatrical performance they had witnessed, I had almost to hold them, to prevent them going off in ecstasies. I never saw any body enjoy anything half as well as they enjoyed the whole show at Barnums. I would not have given three straws to have seen the whole concern, in fact if alone could not have been hired to stay the show out. But I enjoyed it in company with the boys as well as they did. . . . I shall take them to New York tomorrow.

John B. Lamar to Mary Ann Cobb

Macon, December 3, 1850

I expect to be in Athens on Monday. I shall bring you a carriage driver to wit Burton son of Clarissa. He is represented by white & black, to be the steadiest, old-fashioned chap on the plantation. He is healthy & able to work & very willing too. I have lectured him to be very careful not to contract a disease peculiar to young gentleman, of any hue, on emerging from a rustic life into the gay world—namely—"the Big-head." By which I led him to infer, that I meant a self consequence whose premonitory symptoms are, thinking himself more knowing than his owners, & a desire to act as he pleases. And whose latter state is taking the road from Athens back to Baldwin, with his stick & wallet, to resume the labours of the plough on a plantation. He thinks he will do. And I hope his opinion is correct. If he is mistaken however, just let me know & I will send another in his place.

Mary Ann Cobb to Howell Cobb

Athens, December 9, 1850

I received a letter from brother John on Saturday. He will be here to day, and bring with him a carriage driver for us. Burton, a son of Clarissa, Old Jenny's grandson, and also Grandson to Old Charles Walker & Seny, brother John's right hand man & woman—Good stock on both sides for work etc. He is 16 or 17 yrs of age, and brother John represents him as being very steady, but has warned him if he takes the disease called the "Big head" on coming to town, he will walk back to the plantation.

From a remark Bob made to the boys when they told him that Burton would drive the carriage, I think he has no idea of returning to his old home. I shall however feel bound to tell Tom when we have no use for Bob, as he kindly sent him to me in my need, with the assertion that I ought keep him as long as I needed him.

I must do this, tho as far as I am concerned Bob is welcome to remain as long as suits him. The additional Expense that he will be to you in clothes or food will be small, when we remember that he has always been a favored servant.

Howell Cobb to Mary Ann Cobb

Washington, D.C., December 13, 1850

I hope your new carriage driver may prove worthy of his promotion. If he does not, he must expect to return "*to private life*" at the Hurricane. It will be necessary for you to keep Bob until he can learn him how to drive & take care of the horses, carriage &c. Now I hardly know what to say should be done with the old fellow after that. Tom & Sister Marion are certainly entitled to him. . . . But I am free to say, that I am perfectly willing, indeed it would be a source of pleasure to me, to provide for him in his old age. I am more attached to him than any negro, I know, and he is no doubt more attached to me for [a] variety of reasons, principally because I travelled with Papa & him more than any of the other children.

John B. Lamar to Mary Ann Cobb

Macon, January 5, 1854

During the Christmas I had a house full of visitors all the time, half my negroes from Sumter & as many of yours came up to sell their cotton & do their trading. They all lodged & boarded at my house & if I hadn't had an Athens cold to draw my attention from their noise, I should have thought myself in Bedlam. But the cold prevented me from being much troubled with them, as it claimed all my spare thoughts. So you see there is some comfort in a cold, sometimes.

John B. Lamar to Mary Ann Cobb

Macon, November 11, 1854

Your man Alfred has been at the Hurricane for some weeks to go to Athens with Lawrence & the cart when he comes.

Sarah Rootes Cobb to Mary Ann Cobb

Athens, April 3, 1855

All the negroes were well, Alfred got back on sunday morning from the plantation, Johnny has the list of the articles he brought.

John A. Cobb II to Mary Ann Cobb

Athens, April 9, 1855

Alfred went to the plantation a day or two after you left and returned in little over four days. He brought the lard and some old butter but no fresh. I will enclose the overseers letter which he sent by Alfred.

Mary Ann Cobb to John A. Cobb II

Washington, D.C., August 20, 1858

Who is Lawrence hired to? If to Mr Chase and he wishes him another year, let him remain, but if he does not want him, send him to the plantation. Mr. Chase's is the only place I would let him stay at, because there are few servants kept there, and Mr & Mrs. C are both particular and exacting. Lawrence is a "sly rascal," and a year or two under an overseer would do him good.

John B. Lamar to Mary Ann Lamar Cobb[35]

Macon, January 13, 1859

I have this day sent to the express office to be forwarded to you a ten gallon keg of Georgia syrup. . . . I saw the cane cut & crushed in the mill & the syrup boiled myself, as I happened on the plantation when the negroes were at work at it. It was part of their own crop, & I bought it from one of them. They made a fine crop of it last year, every family made a barrel full & some two or three barrels of 30 gallons each.

Mary Ann Cobb to Howell Cobb Jr.

Athens, May 13, 1859

"Turnip Seed" is here, and making himself generally useful.[36] He brought up the new carriage *three* horses, 2 dogs, 'Stansil' & 'Barwick,' A negro woman to nurse Lizzie, the nurse's baby, a pretty fat baby, skin as black and smooth as black satin and the nurse's baby's nurse! quite a cavalcade!!

Loueza[37] to John B. Lamar

Macon, September 2, 1860

Dear Sir,

We are all well at this present time and getting along first rate. I have been to the Indian Springs and stayed four weeks and I would like to go back and stay untill you send for me if you will send me some money. I have not been to Mr. Prince's yet as I liked the spring so very much [while] I stayed thare. If you are wiling write to Young, and let me know

---

35. Mary Ann Lamar Cobb, the eldest daughter of Howell and Mary Ann. To distinguish her from her mother, we always identify her by her full name.

36. "Turnip Seed" was the nickname of the enslaved young man Henry Darby, son of Jim Darby. He had transported the wet nurse Esther to Athens to nurse Mary Ann and Howell's infant daughter, Elizabeth Craig Cobb.

37. Loueza, spelled "Louisa" in documents written by John B. Lamar, was the head housekeeper of Lamar's Macon home. Cobb-Erwin-Lamar Family Collection.

for I would like to stay up thare untill you ar ready to come home for uncle Davey can put the carpets down without me you told me to remind you of the carpet on the stair steps also breakfast plates & cream mug.

I now come to a close.

>Yours respectably,
>Loueza

Jenny Lamar to Mary Ann Cobb[38]

Milledgeville, 1863

My dear Missis,

I write to let you know I have not forgoten you and if you plese mam send your old servant some sugar and coffee and give my love to all the children. I am so disable to come. I send these few lines by Warren. Please send wat you can spare by him to me and you will oblige me for I do love my coffee. Give my love to all my collord friends in the yard and recive the greates portions for yourself.

So farwell till I her from you. I remain your mammy.

---

38. Cobb-Erwin-Lamar Family Collection.

CHAPTER 2

"Those Who Are Dependent upon Us and Completely in Our Power"

AFTER A LIFETIME OF ENSLAVEMENT, Bob Scott had grown both old and bald. For decades he had labored as John Addison Cobb's body servant, traveling across the state with him and young Howell as they supervised the family's plantations and other business interests. Bob had overseen the Cobbs' residences, managed their affairs, and helped raise their children. The family had taken his physical prowess, his energy, and, most poignantly, his time. Freedom may have been beyond the scope of possibility for the elderly man, but now, in the winter of his life, Bob wanted a wig.

As Christmas 1844 approached, John Addison and his wife, Sarah, their children and grandchildren, and more than a dozen enslaved house servants huddled together at the family's thousand-acre Cowpens Plantation in the rolling hills of Walton County, Georgia. Sarah mentioned Bob's request in a letter to her daughter-in-law Mary Ann, who, along with an enslaved woman named Sylvia, had recently joined Howell in Washington, D.C. "Bob asked me today . . . ," she wrote, "to ask you to tell Sylvia not to forget his wig she was to get for him." Sarah was not simply and mindlessly sending Sylvia on an errand in the nation's capital but had clearly given the question of Bob's hairpiece some thought. "I wish if she does get one she may get red hair," she suggested, before glibly noting, "I think it is getting to high times when the negroes wear wigs."[1]

---

1. Sarah Rootes Cobb to Mary Ann Cobb, December 8, 1844. On hairstyle and clothing as a means of resistance against what Stephanie M. H. Camp referred to as the "badge of slavery," as well as assertions of pride and self-expression, see Stephanie M. H. Camp, "The Pleasures of Resistance: Enslaved Women and Body Politics in the Plantation South, 1830–1861," *Journal of Southern History* 68, no. 3 (August 2002): 535–40, 544, 561; Stephanie M. H. Camp, *Closer to Freedom: Enslaved Women and Everyday Resistance in the Plantation South* (Chapel Hill: University of North Carolina Press, 2004), 78–87. See also Kathleen M. Hilliard, *Masters, Slaves, and Exchange: Power's Purchase in the Old South* (New York: Cambridge University Press, 2014), 60–65, 134–40; Katie Knowles, "Fashioning Slavery: Slaves

Making sense of Bob's request, Sarah's consent, and the context and place in which it played out offers a valuable glimpse into the world the enslaved made.[2] The story of Bob's wig comes down to us through three short lines in one letter. It was a trivial occurrence in the lives of the Cobb family, hardly worth note then or now. Yet it provides a frozen moment in which we can see many of the individual players in this book cloistered together, interacting in prosaic ways that reveal the everyday nature of their shared lives, unfiltered and without a sense that history was watching. Those three lines mask an entire universe, and carefully pulling them apart allows us to see and begin to understand the structures and shapes of their world.

Despite Sarah's quip about "negroes wear[ing] wigs," virtually all the residents of the Cowpens that winter had arrived at the plantation bearing the scars of recent events. Family patriarch John Addison Cobb had seen his life's work and substantial fortune slowly turned to dust in the wake of the financial panic that swept the nation several years earlier. His grand home in Athens had been taken away in a sheriff's sale, his family's stellar name and reputation had been tarnished, and his bad debts had forced his eldest son into bankruptcy. Sarah struggled to reconcile herself to their loss of wealth and status, bemoaning in a letter to her daughter-in-law, "You cannot tell what a state of mind I am in about our business, I sometimes think about it till I am almost crazy."[3] John and Sarah arrived at the Cowpens searching for a place of respite, to recuperate from their shame in the safety of their family and perhaps to rebuild.

An earlier telling of this history likely would have focused on the removal of the extended Cobb family to the Cowpens Plantation in the early

---

and Clothing in the U.S. South, 1830–1865," PhD diss., Rice University, 2014; Shane White and Graham White, "Slave Hair and African American Culture in the Eighteenth and Nineteenth Centuries," *Journal of Southern History* 61, no. 1 (February 1995): 49–53, 59–66.

2. It is impossible to suggest that this story, or indeed this volume, offers more than a glimpse into the worlds created and inhabited by the enslaved. Still, it is worth noting that some important scholarship has addressed the difficulty and discomfort of attempting to explain slavery as a whole given the vast differences in the lived experiences of the enslaved. John Inscoe insightfully and provocatively addressed this topic head-on, reminding us that we cannot make sense of the forest without examining the trees. Scholars need to mine the small stories and the glimpses they reveal, he writes, for "only at this most intimate level in which we see slaves and masters interacting as individuals within very particular settings and circumstances can we fully appreciate the contradictions and variables that so complicate the essence of the 'peculiar institution.'" John C. Inscoe, *Race, War, and Remembrance in the Appalachian South* (Louisville: University of Kentucky Press, 2008), 54, 58–62.

3. Sarah Rootes Cobb to Mary Ann Cobb, April 26, 1842.

1840s and suggested simply that they brought a number of enslaved people with them. Yet Sarah's letters make it possible to identify most of these individuals and something of their stories. More important, carefully piecing through the extant documents provides insights into how those they brought with them weathered the upheavals and losses that had devastated the household. They had not reached the Cowpens through mere serendipity or the unthinking actions of their owners. Rather, they were skilled and careful negotiators who had learned to work within the system in order to survive. The enslaved who succeeded in preserving their place in the household understood that the family strove to retain possession of those individuals they most trusted, while those who had not consistently proven themselves indispensable were more easily sold when the situation required. Bob, for example, had spent decades demonstrating loyalty to John Addison Cobb, a tactic that proved invaluable when it became apparent that all of Cobb's property would be auctioned to pay his debts; Bob's ownership was quietly transferred to another family member.

Understanding this set of experiences makes visible just a small fragment of who Bob was and what he knew at the moment that he asked for a wig. He recognized his favored position, to be sure, but likely could never shake the knowledge that he was a valuable piece of property whose place in the Cobbs' world was always fraught with uncertainty.

Bob was also aware that other enslaved individuals in the household struggled along the same path. For example, just two years earlier he had witnessed the dissolution of George's nuclear family as they were forced to go before the auctioneer's hammer in order to pay Howell's debts. George Carter and his daughter Aggy had followed Bob's lead in demonstrating unswerving loyalty to their owners. They were purchased back by John B., who returned them to his sister, even as the rest of their family was separated and scattered.[4] George and Aggy lived beside Bob at the Cowpens; he knew them for their entire lives and consoled them for their losses, while they, in turn, would have celebrated with him the arrival of his new wig. Likewise, all three would have intimately known the histories, joys, and losses of every other of the roughly one dozen enslaved house servants and their children that the extended Cobb families brought to the plantation that winter. Together this group would have

---

4. George's son Robert Carter was also purchased by John B. Lamar at the same time that he bought George and Aggy. While father and daughter were immediately returned to Mary Ann and Howell's household, Robert was sent to serve Lamar in Macon. The family's story will be addressed more fully in chapter 4.

anxiously watched the pregnancies of Rachel and Ellen and ultimately cheered the arrival of Rachel and Coleman's son, Lucius, and Ellen and Squire's daughter, Mary Polk. They would have despaired with Rachel and her sister Susan that she could not introduce her newest child to her mother, Jenny Lamar, or their other sisters, Becky, Clarissa, and Lavinia, all of whom lived elsewhere in the state. They would have consoled Sylvia's children, Jim, Howard, and Ellick, who were missing their mother since she departed for Washington, D.C. They would have mourned the death of Daniel but perhaps only in secret, as they knew his widow Phyllis had "prayed for it constantly" because "he had served her too bad."[5]

All told, the story of Bob's wig covers over the history, lives, losses, and hopes of the enslaved people who were gathered together at the Cowpens Plantation that winter of 1844–45. Bob, George and Aggy, Rachel and Lucius and her other children, Ellen and Squire and Mary Polk, Susan, Jim, Howard, Ellick, and Phyllis, among others, have stories to tell. Their experiences in slavery were by no means universal to all enslaved, nor did they reflect many who labored within households. Yet it is possible that the ordinary nature of their everyday lives sheds some new light onto the lived experiences of many.

For all they understood about why they wound up at the Cowpens Plantation, they also recognized their places, and the places of their loved ones, within the broader web of connectivity that defined the Cobb-Lamar network as it spanned the state. Bob occupied a central position at the inception of this most remarkable and complicated system. The long story of his enslavement was defined by constant motion. Indeed, in describing his willingness to provide for Bob in his old age, Howell fondly recalled his earliest memories of frequently "travell[ing] with Papa & him," as the two men journeyed near and far.[6] Mary Ann's brother Andrew also recollected him as seemingly ever-present at all of the family's properties, once playfully noting that his sister likely knew about his drunken debauchery in Louisville because, "Bob Scott has probable already *told* you of it."[7] Howell's cousin Sarah Prince more graciously remarked, "There are not many recollections of my past life in which his form is not conspicuously presented to my mind's eye."[8] For four decades, Bob was a part of the unseen yet perfectly functioning root system that circulated information,

5. Sarah Rootes Cobb to Mary Ann Cobb, December 1, 1845.
6. Howell Cobb to Mary Ann Cobb, December 13, 1850.
7. Andrew Lamar to Mary Ann Cobb, January 4, 1838.
8. Sarah Prince to Mary Ann Cobb, January 6, 1854.

material goods, financial and intellectual capital, and people among the family's Georgia plantations.

As the family's holdings expanded and Bob aged, the pathways of transportation and communication became more complex. By the 1840s, George Carter had been brought into the system to learn at Bob's side. Alfred followed in the 1850s. Others also participated in the transmission of information as they moved or were moved between plantations or back and forth between plantations and town. The enslaved who were literate contributed directly by writing to family members. Those who were illiterate occasionally relied on others to draft letters on their behalf. All the while, an endless barrage of correspondence moved between members of the Cobb-Lamar family, more formally carrying notices of people and events. Sarah and Mary Ann managed vast quantities of information from their writing desks, taking what they heard through the informal network maintained by Bob and others and writing it out, as well as taking in what came through formal communications and passing it along to other enslaved people. This complicated ecosystem provided for the constant transmission of news of the daily lives of the enslaved, crucially ensuring the survival of emotional bonds between those who otherwise would have been disconnected, and reminding them that they were part of a world that extended beyond the boundaries of any given plantation.[9]

It is not mere conjecture to suggest that the enslaved would have understood this network of connectivity. Quite the opposite, they actively engaged with it. For example, Sylvia and her three sons were brought to the Cowpens. Her daughters Polly and Eliza were sent to be with their

---

9. For the ability of the enslaved to create worlds that extended beyond the boundaries of a given plantation, see Anthony E. Kaye, *Joining Places: Slave Neighborhoods of the Old South* (Chapel Hill: University of North Carolina Press, 2007), 34–45, 156–57, 162–64. See also Daina Ramey Berry, *Swing the Sickle for the Harvest Is Ripe: Gender and Slavery in Antebellum Georgia* (Champaign: University of Illinois Press, 2007), 54–56, 60–75; Antoinette T. Jackson, *Speaking for the Enslaved: Heritage Interpretation at Antebellum Plantation Sites* (Walnut Creek, Calif.: Left Coast Press, 2012), 21–27; Lorena S. Walsh, *From Calabar to Carter's Grove: The History of a Virginia Slave Community* (Charlottesville: University of Virginia Press, 1997), 49–52; and Charles Joiner, *Down by the Riverside: A South Carolina Slave Community* (Urbana: University of Illinois Press, 1984), 129–32. For the ways in which the enslaved constructed kinship and social boundaries around their own communities and limited who counted as one of their own, see Dylan C. Penningroth, *The Claims of Kinfolk: African American Property and Community in the Nineteenth-Century South* (Chapel Hill: University of North Carolina Press, 2003), 87–89; and Emily West, "The Debate on the Strength of Slave Families: South Carolina and the Importance of Cross-Plantation Marriages," *Journal of American Studies* 33, no. 2 (August 1999): 222–23, 234–39.

grandmother, Old Polly Flagg, at Cherry Hill.[10] Howell and Mary Ann's removal to Washington, D.C., further strained these ties. When Sylvia accompanied them as a nursemaid, and was tasked with acquiring a wig for Bob, it came at the cost of leaving all of her children behind. The Cobbs were aware of, even sympathetic to, the strain caused by this forced separation. Sarah Cobb asked her daughter-in-law to "give our love to Sylvia and tell her Jim is well."[11] John B. Lamar told Howell to pass along that "Polly and Eliza [were] well."[12] Another family member reported, "I saw [Sylvia's son] Howard in Macon he was taken with Scarlet Fever . . . and came very near dying, but was up waiting about the table the day I left."[13] The full extent of the interplay between the informal and formal networks of communication is clear in a note from Howell's sister, reminding Mary Ann to "tell Aunt Sylvia that Andrew's boy had just returned from Jefferson and told Aggy that Polly and Eliza and her mother were quite well."[14] To be clear, for this information to reach its destination it had to be told by Polly, Eliza, and Old Polly at Cherry Hill to the enslaved courier of Andrew Lamar, who then traveled 115 miles to repeat it to Aggy at the Cowpens, who in turn conveyed it to Howell's sister, who then relayed it in a letter to Mary Ann, so that it could be shared with Sylvia.

Yet Sylvia and other enslaved people did not rely on the network merely for communication. They also employed it in attempts to manipulate their places and those of their family members within it. By constantly seeking information from Mary Ann and John B. about the health

10. Aggy's mother was named "Sylva," and she had sisters named "Polly" and "Eliza." Aggy's mother and sisters were sold at auction in 1842. None of them are mentioned in the subsequent sale notice of September 1843. The vast preponderance of evidence suggests that they were completely different individuals than the Sylvia who was moved to Cowpens Plantation and the Polly and Eliza who were moved to Cherry Hill Plantation. Moreover, there are repeated instances when Mary Ann explicitly identified George and Robert as Aggy's father and brother. She also explicitly and repeatedly identified Sylvia as the mother of Polly and Eliza. Nowhere, over decades of writing, did she ever suggest any family connection between Aggy and Sylvia, Polly, or Eliza. A letter Aggy wrote on November 2, 1857, however, confounds the issue. In that document, Aggy asked Howell Jr. to relay greetings to "mama and polly and elisar." While this request would seem to imply that Aggy was referring to Sylvia as her mother, and Polly and Eliza as her sisters, it is more likely that she alluded to the children calling Sylvia "mama." Indeed, as evidenced by a letter from 1861, Mary Ann mentioned how young Lizzie Cobb called Aggy "Marmer." Furthermore, in a letter from March, 1857, Aggy referred to Sylvia as "ant silve."

11. Sarah Rootes Cobb to Mary Ann Cobb, February 25, 1844.
12. John B. Lamar to Howell Cobb, May 15, 1844.
13. Williams Rutherford to Howell Cobb, February 17, 1845.
14. Mary Willis Cobb to Mary Ann Cobb, March 6, 1844.

and location of her children, she reminded them of the price she paid for serving the family so faithfully.[15] Mary Ann, missing her own sons, also left behind at the Cowpens, might have felt more sympathetic to Sylvia's plight than she otherwise would have been. This shared longing for absent family probably contributed to an unusual promise. Mary Ann, who already intended to bring Sylvia's daughter Eliza to Athens, promised to bring Polly as well. Despite her brother's protest that removing Old Polly's last relative from Cherry Hill would manifest "a selfish disregard for an aged parent," Mary Ann insisted otherwise, writing, "It is well to gratify servants sometimes, and better still to make good your promises to them, as it holds out to them in return a certain reward."[16]

Sylvia saw a rare opportunity to collect on a promise and define the reward. Seeking to restore further the integrity of her family unit, she immediately launched a covert campaign to bring her mother to Athens. Mary Ann learned of the conspiracy between Sylvia and Old Polly while visiting Cherry Hill. Another enslaved laborer on the plantation related details of the plan to Mary Ann who, in turn, shared the information with her maidservant, Aggy Carter. Aggy then informed James Stewart, an enslaved servant in the Cobb household, who confronted Old Polly with a warning from their mistress. Mary Ann complained of Sylvia's "plotting" in a letter to her husband, asserting, "I assume she acquired a fondness for maneuvering during her intercourse with the messes at Washington, and thinks to benefit herself by her knowledge." She ominously repeated the warning she had Aggy pass along to James Stewart, who passed it to Old Polly, that "Sylvia if she does not look sharp to her ways will wake up some morning and find herself the owner of a snug little log hut at the Harris place, with the office of chief cook to the overseer, for I will not be imposed upon any further."[17] While she had succeeded in reuniting with her daughters in Athens, Sylvia heeded Mary Ann's warning and abandoned her efforts on her mother's behalf. Old Polly remained at Cherry

---

15. Sylvia invoked a "standard of respectable womanhood," by which elite women expected that gender norms and maternal roles applied even to enslaved women, to manipulate Mary Ann into reuniting her with her children. Camp, *Closer to Freedom*, 37–38. See also James Oakes, *Slavery and Freedom: An Interpretation of the Old South* (New York: W. W. Norton, 1990), 150–52.

16. John B. Lamar to Mary Ann Cobb, December 28, 1848; Mary Ann Cobb to Howell Cobb, January 10, 1849.

17. Mary Ann Cobb to Howell Cobb, January 15, 1849. John B. Lamar, acting as trustee for his sister, purchased the Harris Place Plantation, which adjoined the Hurricane Plantation, in March 1845.

Hill. Sylvia's skill in knowing when to push had enabled her to partially reunite her family, but knowing when to relent allowed her to preserve her place in the Cobb household.

Like Sylvia, Rachel Lamar Cole and her mother, Jenny Lamar, negotiated within the network to secure whatever advantages they could for their family. Rachel initially benefited from her mother's place of esteem in the Cobb-Lamar family. Jenny had gained the family's affection as a nursemaid to John B., Mary Ann, and Andrew and later been granted by Zachariah Lamar both a house and an exemption from further labor.[18] By the 1840s, the family had come to depend on Rachel for her skill with a needle and thread. Sarah Cobb commended her to Mary Ann as a "first-rate seamstress" and noted that it would be "a serious loss . . . to have to give up [her] sewing."[19]

Relocation to the Cowpens meant that Rachel had to be separated from her husband, Coleman Cole, who remained with his owners, the Hull family, thirty miles away in Athens. The couple relied on the network to remain in contact and periodically visited back and forth. Mary Ann recorded the birth of Rachel and Coleman's son, Lucius, in her account book, as she did for Rachel's nine other children.[20] News of the birth also would have spread through the informal pathways suggested above. Jenny Lamar almost certainly learned of her newest grandson's arrival by these means. She got to know her grandchildren as a result of Rachel being allowed to make annual Christmas visits to the Hurricane Plantation, near the home Mary Ann provided Jenny in Milledgeville. News of Rachel, her children, and Coleman, their health, and their time with one another appeared in Mary Ann's letters for the next twenty years.

Jenny and Rachel generally conformed to expectations but occasionally made a misstep, leaving Mary Ann to judge that both needed to be more compliant. Mary Ann had generally responded favorably, or at least allowed some concessions, when appealed to directly and forthrightly regarding family considerations of the enslaved. She had done as much when Sylvia requested to have her daughters brought to Athens. Likewise, she consented to Jenny Lamar's November 1854 petition to have her newborn granddaughter, a child of Becky, moved to Jenny's house in

18. *Federal Union* (Milledgeville), July 13, 1869.
19. Sarah Rootes Cobb to Mary Ann Cobb, August 1, 1845; Sarah Rootes Cobb to Mary Ann Cobb, May 4, 1845.
20. Mary Lamar Cobb Account Book, Hargrett Rare Book and Manuscript Library, University of Georgia, Athens.

Milledgeville. In December 1848, Mary Ann acceded to Rachel's request and encouraged Howell to agree to hiring Rachel's enslaved husband, Coleman, as a carpenter. A year later, in December 1849, she agreed to have Rachel and Coleman's nine-year-old son, Bob, brought back to Athens from a blacksmithing apprenticeship in Milledgeville so that he could be with his mother. Yet, as Sylvia and Old Polly learned when their covert efforts were exposed, Mary Ann could respond fiercely when she feared that the people she enslaved were communicating behind her back about how to manipulate her. Jenny Lamar and Rachel inadvertently stepped over this invisible line in 1855, when Mary Ann learned that Jenny had written to Rachel bemoaning Rachel's separation from her children. Mary Ann recoiled in anger and declared "I wish they were *all* in Liberia. (I mean my old nurse & family)."[21] Ill will continued to simmer. The following year Mary Ann ranted, "I cannot endure the idea of going through life with such an incubus, as she and her family have become by their worthlessness and insolence."[22]

Years of frustration with Rachel prompted Mary Ann to consider removing her from the household and dispatching her to the plantation. The breaking point came when she learned that Rachel and Coleman had covertly negotiated to hire their eldest daughter, Sabina, into service with the Hull family. Incredulously she asked Howell, "What do you think of this assumption of authority on the part of Rachel and Coleman? We *must* ship them from the lot, or our whole household will be in insubordination. The plantation is the place for Rachel and tribe."[23] Rachel may have enjoyed annual visits to family and friends on the Hurricane but felt no desire to reside there permanently.[24] As a result, Sabina was returned to the Cobbs, and Rachel embarked on a three-month campaign to re-

---

21. Mary Ann Cobb to Howell Cobb, June 4, 1855.

22. Mary Ann Cobb to Howell Cobb, January 11, 1856.

23. Mary Ann Cobb to Howell Cobb, January 9, 1857.

24. On the fluidity between house and field labor and how the enslaved viewed the distinction, see Berry, *Swing the Sickle for the Harvest Is Ripe*, 35–51; Michael Strutt, "Slave Housing on Antebellum Tennessee," in *Cabin, Quarter, Plantation: Architecture and Landscapes of North American Slavery*, ed. Clifton Ellis and Rebecca Ginsburg (New Haven: Yale University Press, 2010), 230–31; Peter Kolchin, *American Slavery, 1619–1877* (New York: Hill and Wang, 1993), 53–54, 107–11; Elizabeth Fox-Genovese, *Within the Plantation Household: Black and White Women of the Old Plantation South* (Chapel Hill: University of North Carolina Press, 1988), 152–53, 167; Paul D. Escott, *Slavery Remembered: A Record of Twentieth-Century Slave Narratives* (Chapel Hill: University of North Carolina Press, 1979), 59–61; Leon F. Litwack, *Been in the Storm So Long: The Aftermath of Slavery* (New York: Knopf, 1979), 156–57; Eugene Genovese, *Roll, Jordan, Roll: The World the Slaves Made* (New York: Pantheon Books, 1974), 328–42.

gain her status within the household. She almost succeeded, but time
worked against her. Howell's appointment as secretary of the treasury in
early 1857 forced Mary Ann to determine who would attend the family in
Washington and who would be sent to the plantations. Rachel was left behind. Mary Ann praised her intelligence and recent cooperative attitude
but decided that others were more loyal and obedient. "If *she* only possessed Sylvia or Aggys disposition," she wrote, "I would not leave Georgia
without her."[25] Rachel succeeded in delaying her departure for the Hurricane for a little over a year, but once she was sent to the plantation she
does not appear to have ever worked in the Cobb household again.

No one in the Cobb-Lamar orbit proved as adept at reading the ac-
tions of the enslaved and the reactions of their masters as did George
Carter and his daughter, Aggy. Careful observation of the experiences of
Bob, Sylvia, and Rachel, among the hundreds of other enslaved people
George saw in his travels as a courier, established useful lessons that the
Carters employed to make their own lives more bearable. Although his
owners failed to see it, George's life story is a testament to his belief—and
Bob's—that constant demonstrations of fidelity were the only path to security in an inherently unjust and transient system.[26] He passed these lessons on to his daughter, who in turn surpassed even her father in ensuring that her "disposition" never caused the Cobb-Lamars to doubt her
loyalty or question her integrity. Indeed, Mary Ann, her husband, and
her brother appear almost willfully blind to the extent to which George
and Aggy were learning to quietly work the system to their advantage.

George and Aggy arrived at the Cowpens having recently endured a
life-changing personal tragedy. Howell's debts had placed George, his
wife, and their six children on the auction block in 1842 and again in
1843. Ultimately only father and daughter were returned to Howell and
Mary Ann because of their vital roles in the operation of the household.
Their ability to withstand such a devastating trial is a testament to the wis-
dom George had been learning from Bob for years. He knew that if he
wished to persevere, to stay beside his remaining child, he had to do as he
always had and follow Bob's model of both duty and disposition. He was
rewarded with the trusted position of courier, a role that brought with it
a certain level of autonomy as he freely moved goods and information

---

25. Mary Ann Cobb to Howell Cobb, June 17, 1857.

26. Anthony Kaye, *Joining Places*, 88–89; Erskine Clarke, *Dwelling Place: A Plantation Epic*
(New Haven: Yale University Press, 2005), 187–88, 229, 305–7, 362–63, 373; Fox-Genovese,
Within the Plantation Household, 307–8; Escott, *Slavery Remembered*, 31–35, 74–75.

between the family's plantations. He was also intermittently hired out, usually as a house servant to one of the Cobbs' neighbors, but always remained close within the geographic and social networks of his daughter.

George may have reconciled himself to his position and the security it seems to have brought. Or maybe he did not. Perhaps he had so mastered the ability to mask his festering resentment for the people who sold his family that the Cobbs never recorded him as anything but compliant and content. In any case, and no matter who instigated it, it is bewildering to find that by 1850 the Cobbs had sold George to Charles McCay, a professor of mathematics at the University of Georgia and the same neighbor who had previously hired him.[27]

In 1853 McCay accepted a position at the University of South Carolina. George had clearly struggled with being separated from his family, but this further removal to Columbia proved unbearable. McCay offered to sell him back to the Cobbs but at an inflated price. The Cobbs declined the offer. Within two years, however, George, older and now suffering a debilitating illness, "expressed his anxiety to have some of his children with him."[28] He asked McCay to purchase his son, Nelson, but McCay explained that he had no need for additional house servants.[29] Reluctant to bear the expense of caring for the ailing man, McCay once again offered to sell him back to the Cobbs so he could be near his daughter. Mary Ann resented her former neighbor's attempt to sell her back "a *diseased negro*," but her response to the renewed offer was that she and Howell ought to repay his lifetime of labor, as they had for Bob, with "kindness and care." "Even if he could do no more than clean boots," she wrote, it seemed fitting to her that George's "old age might be passed in the society of his children."[30]

It is illustrative to consider this situation in light of the simultaneous events surrounding Rachel and her family. Mary Ann's thoughts on

27. There is no record of exactly when the sale took place. It is possible that it was the result of the lingering consequences of Howell's bankruptcy. Letters demonstrate, however, that George was with McCay in 1846—whether hired or sold is not evident—but back with the Cobbs again later in the decade and in the early 1850s.

28. Mary Ann Cobb to Howell Cobb, June 17, 1857.

29. There is no evidence that Nelson had remained within the Cobb-Lamar network, but McCay's letter makes clear that the Carters at least knew of his whereabouts.

30. Mary Ann Cobb to Howell Cobb, November 6, 1855. See also John B. Lamar to Mary Ann Cobb, February 2, 1835. On the circumstances of elderly and disabled enslaved people, see Daina Ramey Berry, "Elderly and Superannuated," chap. 5 in *The Price for Their Pound of Flesh* (Boston: Beacon Press, 2017); Stacy K. Close, *Elderly Slaves of the Plantation South* (New York: Garland, 1997); Joiner, *Down by the Riverside*, 63–65; Genovese, *Roll, Jordan, Roll*, 32.

George's return ran parallel to her concurrent railing against Rachel as an "incubus" from a family defined by "worthlessness and insolence." Where Rachel could never fully convince Mary Ann that she had not had her hand on the strings, the Carters appear to have learned well and maneuvered toward a different outcome. Aggy had certainly heard Mary Ann's thoughts and mapped out her judgments when a similar situation had unfolded around Sylvia several years earlier. She remained closer in physical proximity to Mary Ann than any other person during the months of unrest over Rachel and her family. Where the others clumsily challenged Mary Ann's authority, Aggy absorbed the lessons and presented herself as truthful and compliant throughout the entire ordeal.

Seen through this new lens, Mary Ann's decree that Rachel would have been saved from banishment to the plantation had she possessed Aggy's "disposition" is telling. Aggy's ability to walk a fine line between her own desires and those of Mary Ann clearly affected what ultimately happened with her father. When questioned by Mary Ann about his health, Aggy honestly reported that it had been deteriorating for some time. Her agreeable behavior solidified Mary Ann's willingness to fulfill her wish. Even after it became apparent that George suffered from what she called a "loathsome" disease, rather than the rheumatism that McCay described, Mary Ann was willing to consider that she might have "to give up Aggy entirely to attend to him."[31] George was purchased and brought back to live near his daughter in Athens. Aggy likely cared for him as was necessary, but it appears that other enslaved people were also put to the task in order to preserve her focus on the needs of Mary Ann and her children. Howell applauded his wife's resolution of the situation to "gratify both George and Aggy," without ever seeing that either George or Aggy had any role in the decision.[32]

The stories of Aggy and George, Sylvia, Rachel, and Bob reveal a world far broader than the five people at its center. Those five were connected both to one another and to hundreds of unseen others in a vast and complex ecosystem. Their stories only begin to hint at the kind of symbiotic relationships that existed between all of the Cobb-Lamar people and places, near and far. The majority of people owned by the family were not isolated and disconnected but lived lives shaped by the knowledge that they were bound together as part of a larger community. Their world

31. Mary Ann Cobb to Howell Cobb, January 17, 1856.
32. Howell Cobb to Mary Ann Cobb, January 17, 1856.

may have spanned urban and plantation landscapes separated by hundreds of miles, but their relationships survived and flourished along the same pathways by which material goods and information flowed back and forth.

The ability to maintain this community, however, carried with it an intrinsic understanding of the fluidity that existed between assignments to the households or the plantations, as well as the mutability of one's position and rank within the system. All involved tried to wield it to their advantage. Not all succeeded. Yet the stories relayed here offer an opening onto the lives of hundreds of enslaved others whose experiences may have differed by degree from the events described but who would have understood their larger meanings. Bob, Sylvia, Rachel, Aggy, and George saw these happenings as crucial moments in their lives at the time. Like all their counterparts, they would perhaps have recognized themselves and their community in this telling far more than they would have in a traditional accounting of slavery as seen through a record of labor, calories provided and consumed, clothing allotments, access to medical care, or physical violence. These fragments of their stories suggest a way of uncovering at least a fleeting glimpse of who they were, who they thought about, the struggles they faced, where they wanted to be and what they wanted to be doing, their small fears and larger goals, and how they made meaningful lives within—or despite—the confines imposed upon them.

John B. Lamar to Mary Ann Cobb
Milledgeville, February 4, 1835

The sale of fathers unwilled property has just this day been concluded. The negroes were sold yesterday at the Courthouse & taking into consideration, their inferiority & age (being such as father would not will to us) they brought good prices. . . .

I purchased 4 of the old negroes & a deformed boy. They were so unwilling to leave the family that I took them although they will be of no value.

Old Izeal & Delaide have children belonging to you & I shall let the old creatures remain at the Cedar Shoals near their children, in the house they formerly occupied when that place was cultivated. Old Ben Putnam

I shall carry home with me, to raise hogs & to keep up the fences around my swamp fields. Old Hannah shall raise me chickens. Ben is a widower of 60 & Hannah a widow of the same charming age. I am going to try to effect a match. Luke the deformed boy is rather much of an idiot to make anything of. However as I owned his father & mother (valuable negroes) I could not bear to see him separated from them.

Howell Cobb to Mary Ann Cobb

Milledgeville, February 2, 1837

Aunt Jenny is now in the room all are well with her and I am now making arrangements to buy her husband.

Howell Cobb to Mary Ann Cobb

Milledgeville, May 7, 1839

Aunt Jenny & people are all well. I have made an offer for her husband but dont know whether it will be accepted or not.

Mary Ann Cobb to Howell Cobb

Athens, April 17, 1842

Susan commenced growing worse the fourth day after the birth of her child, and on tuesday she was so ill that I concluded it was best for me to send for Aunt Patsy.[33] I sent Bob & the carriage for her on wednesday, since then she has had to visit Susan nearly every hour each day. . . .

Today she is some better, her mouth is touched with calomel, and the Doctor thinks she may recover with a great deal of care. She is very low indeed and poor thing even through all her pain and suffering she does not forget the impending separation from her Mistress. . . .

Aggy's health has been declining for several months past, and with

---

33. Nickname for Martha Rootes Jackson, the sister of Sarah Rootes Cobb and wife of William H. Jackson. They lived next door to Sarah and John A. Cobb at the Cowpens.

Aunt Patsy's advice I have put her under Dr. Moore's[34] care. She is now confined to bed. I will tell you her complaint when I see you. It is one that must receive immediate relief, or the consequences will prove fatal.

Sarah Rootes Cobb to Mary Ann Cobb

Cowpens Plantation, February 25, 1844

Give our love to Sylvia & tell her Jim is well they had a party here last night. The supper was at Rachel's house.

Sarah Rootes Cobb to Mary Ann Cobb[35]

Cowpens Plantation, April 1, 1844

Today we sent Howard back to Mr. Jackson, he was so unwilling to go, it made me feel very sorry for him. . . . John Grant happening to be at Col Jackson's I went over *to see him,* and asked him to befriend Howard if any bad treatment was givin him, which he promised me he would do.

Sarah Rootes Cobb to Mary Ann Cobb

Cowpens Plantation, April 24, 1844

I wrote you I had put Rachel to spinning . . . three hanks and then [she] told me it had brought on her old complaint, and she wished me to let you know it, I stopt her at once, and gave her some of my sewing to do, till I could hear from you, what you would wish her to do, as I knew you would not make her spin if it had that effect upon her, her Bob[36] has been sick but has got quite well again.

---

34. Richard Dudley Moore (May 20, 1809–October 31, 1873), an Athens physician whom the Cobbs frequently employed. Moore College at the University of Georgia is named in his honor.

35. Sarah added this note about Sylvia's son Howard at the end of a letter written by her daughter, Mary Willis Cobb.

36. Son of Rachel and Coleman Cole.

John B. Lamar to Howell Cobb

Macon, May 15, 1844

Tell Aunt Sylvia that Polly and Eliza are well & look as lively as two crickets. Polly's occupation is to carry water in the fields to the hands. Eliza amuses herself by driving up the cows, & turning out the calves, and has learned to sing out like an old drover. They seem so pleased with life at Cherry hill, that I think they will be unwilling to exchange it for a residence at the Cowpens or Athens when their mistress comes home.

Sarah Rootes Cobb to Mary Ann Cobb

Cowpens Plantation, December 8, 1844

Ellen had a fine daughter last night and there was not a creature in the house with her but Squire when the child was born, she was complaining a good deal in the afternoon, and I wanted to send for [the midwife] but she would not agree to it, she and the child are both doing well. . . . Rachel . . . helped me some about our meat . . . she and her children are well.

Sarah Rootes Cobb to Mary Ann Cobb

Cowpens Plantation, December 18, 1844

Howell & John A. were collecting the hoofs Bob took off the hogs feet, in cleaning them for souse and said they were going to put them on old Jacob [a horse] for shoes. . . .

Bob asked me today when I wrote to you, to ask you to tell Sylvia not to forget his wig she was to get for him, I wish if she does get one she may get red hair, I think it is getting to high times when the negroes wear wigs.

Sarah Rootes Cobb to Mary Ann Cobb

Cowpens Plantation, January 12, 1845

Ellens baby is very sick. It was taken friday night. It is now I hope a little better tho still a very sick child. . . .

Bob told me he went all over your house when he was in Athens, and it was as clean as a penny and one of the nicest fixed houses & lot he ever saw. . . . Rachel and her children were well, she had a rising on one of her fingers and sent me word it kept her from going on very fast with her sewing, Sylvia is very well and she & Jim Stuart are very comfortably settled in Rachel's old house, she is very attentive to the boys & they are very fond of her. . . .

All the servants beg to be remembered to you Howell & the boys & love to Aggy.

Sarah Rootes Cobb [writing for John A. Cobb II] to Mary Ann Cobb

Cowpens Plantation, January 15, 1845

I told Mammy Sibby[37] what Mrs Ritter[38] said and that her other old acquaintances had enquired about her, and it pleased her very much to see she was not forgotten, I think she would not dislike another trip to Washington, she often talks about what took place when she was there. . . .

Aunt Ellens baby is nearly well and all the rest on the plantation keep well.

Sarah Rootes Cobb to Mary Ann Cobb

Cowpens Plantation, December 1, 1845

Big Lucy & Betty are both sick with bad colds, Sylvia has got over hers, Ellick has been down to see her, and stayed several days, he has grown to be a large man, James & his wife were both here yesterday, she spins as

---

37. Sylvia.
38. Wife of John Ritter, U.S. congressman from Pennsylvania.

much in a day as Ellen does, as she cleans up the room in the morning where we sleep, Rachel gets along very well with her work, she is on the last jacket, and will then commence the shirts, her husband was here yesterday, his brother Lucius has lost his wife, a woman of Mrs Goldings, they had been married but a short time, Daniel Phillis's old husband is dead, and Phillis says she thanks God for it, for she prayed for it constantly, she said she heard he died very happy, and she hopes he did, but he had served her too bad. . . .

I told Bob today to feed [Spot the cow] well and take good care of her for you, and he promised to do it. Sylvia seemed much pleased that she was remembered by Mr & Mrs Bowlin.[39]

Sarah Rootes Cobb to Mary Ann Cobb

McDonough, May 4, 1845

It is a serious loss to you to have to give up Rachel's sewing I do not know how you will get along without her, Sylvia & Aggy both sew so slow they cannot supply her place, and I have none to offer you.

Mary Ann Cobb to S. M. R. Jackson[40]

Cowpens Plantation, May 9, 1845

Ellen's daughter that she had in the winter is called "Mary Polk." Mary Willis gave the first name, and Squire thru a feeling of democratic enthusiasm I presume added Polk.

39. James Bowlin, U.S. congressman from Missouri, and his wife, Margaret.
40. Sarah Maria Rootes Jackson (1824–97), the daughter of William and Martha Jackson and a cousin of Howell Cobb. She later married Oliver Hillhouse Prince and moved to Athens.

Sarah Rootes Cobb to Mary Ann Cobb

Cowpens Plantation, January 12, [1846][41]

Rachel & Aggy are well and tell Sylvia Jim keeps well and I believe all are well pleased on the rail road,[42] as one or two have been over and say so.

Mary Ann Cobb to Howell Cobb

Athens, April 17, 1846

George has been to see me, and wanted to know how long it would be before he could come home. Tho he is satisfied at Mr. McKays, he says he feels like he wanted to be with us again. I told him if he was in a good situation, he had better be contented to remain there, for I feared it would be out of your power to buy him back.

Jenny Lamar to Mary Ann Cobb

Milledgeville, July 23, 1847

My Dear Mistress,

I have just heard today that you are very low, and I want you to let me know as soon as possible, how it is with you exactly. If I can do anything for you, and you desire to see me, as it is my desire to see you, write to me, and send for me, and I will come. But if we never see each other again in this world, I hope we shall meet in Heaven. Remember my love to your children and to my children. If Miss Mary Ann should not be in place, I want my daughter Rachel to answer this letter at once.

I am pretty well now, but I have been quite poorly with the rheumatism.

---

41. Sarah misdated this letter 1845, but the content makes clear the letter is from January 1846.

42. John Thomas Grant (December 13, 1813–January 18, 1887), the husband of Howell's cousin, hired several enslaved laborers from the Cobb-Lamars to work for his engineering firm, which constructed railroads across the South.

My children at the plantation have been sick, but they are better. Sabina's family are well all but little Wilkes.[43] He is in the same state, he can't walk.

I pray the Lord will enable you to glorify his name, either in life or in death. All power and grace is with him. He can raise you up and make you a burning and a shining light, or he can take you to himself according to his pleasure. Please let me know how you feel. I hope you have a gospel faith in the Saviour. Please pray for me. I am a poor weak creature, nothing without Christ. I want more of his spirit. I wish you would please to let me know how my daughter Susan living in Walton is. I have heard she has been confined lately.

I have no more at present, but remain your aged & faithful servant.

Jenny Lamar

Mary Ann Cobb to Howell Cobb
Athens, December 1848

Lamar is well enough to whip Bob [Cole] with whom he got in a passion just now because Bob refused to mind him, and I have been intrusted the meanwhile to adjust the dispute, Lamar pleading his own case and Howell that of Bob's, on enquiry I found both in fault, and after a lecture to both I dismissed them with separate injunctions that Lamar was never to whip the little negroes but report their disobedience to me, and Bob was to obey his young master.

I am preparing some coarse lumber to build a wash house, which Jim can do with a little assistance from a carpenter and yesterday Coleman, Rachels husband applied for work during Christmas week and as he is on the lot and will be fed anyhow it will be more convenient and economical to employ him here as any other but I did not give him [an] answer until I could hear from you.

If you have no objection to my employing a negro carpenter, and it will not endanger the good cause of democracy my preferences will lead me to employ Coleman. I leave the matter to your judgment, only give me a speedy answer, as he will have to look elsewhere.

---

43. Sabina was the mother of Wilkes Flagg (ca. 1802–November 13, 1878), who married Jenny's daughter, Lavinia. They had one son, Wilkes, about 1830. Sabina, Wilkes, Lavinia, and Jenny were all owned by Zachariah Lamar, who sold all but Jenny to Tomlinson Fort of Milledgeville sometime around 1830.

Mary Ann Cobb to Howell Cobb

Swift Creek Plantation, February 2, 1849

Lamar, myself, Howell & Aggy, all took colds on our way from the Cowpens. . . .

Poor Old Mingo died at the Hurricane the night we reached the Harris place, where we staid, as the house there is large and comfortable.

All the negroes on both places are pretty well with little complaint, except among the standing complainers, being old ones who have a right to do so from having a number of children, with advancing years, such as Old Ben Robinson and his wife Patsy, who Lamar declares is larger than Dixon H Lewis[44] was, and Charity.

The negroes were exceedingly glad to see me and the children, and made many enquiries after you, and were curious to know if you were not tired of going to Washington, and when you were going to quit, and when you are coming to see them, as they are very anxious to see you. I could answer only one question, and that was the first, by telling them your going to Washington interfered with you coming to the plantation. You will have to come some time shortly to gratify them with a sight of you. They have now a very favorable impression of you, as they one and all agreed that Lamar was the prettiest of all the boys, and he was exactly like you, "the very spirit of his papa." One said he had "big fat jowls like you," and another "his long hair stood like yours."

Old Polly Flagg was more politic. She answered that he was mightily like Mass Howell when he was a boy, but he favored his mama too. By the bye Sylvia has been plotting some in connection with Old Polly. I assume she acquired a fondness for maneuvering during her intercourse with the messes at Washington, and thinks to benefit herself by her knowledge. She is assuming to carry her mother to Athens. I am told that this old lady is part of it. Neither of them have breathed it to me, but the old lady thinks she is competent to wash up my dishes, and tend my poultry. Is it not laughable. Sylvia if she does not look sharp to her ways will wake up some morning and find herself the owner of a snug little log hut at the Harris place, with the office of chief cook to the overseer, for I will not be imposed upon any further than having to hire her girls every year, and I

---

44. Dixon Hall Lewis (1802–48) was a US congressman and then senator from Alabama who weighed nearly five hundred pounds.

intend to tell her so as soon as I return. And giving her to understand that she is on probation from this time forth. I feel perfectly indignant at her boldness. Carrying young Polly there to be hired by the year was about as much as I could endure, and not even that if [I] had not foolishly promised it. All obligations are cancelled . . . and she will have to hack it close, or I am mistaken. I would try a cooking stove and stand to it day by day before I would be imposed upon in such a manner. Our Athens household will have to be let down considerably and when you return I shall certainly look to you to cooperate with me in the undertaking. I gathered my information from old Aggy and I told her it was impossible and she will tell the old lady. I understand that James gave the old lady a talk, as he was very much astonished to hear of it from my Aggy whom I had told of it. The old lady is somewhat childish and quarrelled with him for his pains. She is comfortably fixed, and keeps as nice a house as I have seen.

John B. Lamar to John A. Cobb II

Macon, November 8, 1849

I returned home last night just as the supper bell was ringing, from a visit to Sumpter. I found a hat full of letters for me. . . . As I was so anxious to read the letters from Athens & hear the news from you all I concluded to read the letters & let other people have my share of supper.

So I sent Henry & got a quart of oysters just from Savannah by the evening cars, & while he was getting the bread, pepper & other "fixins" from the hotel & was steaming the oysters, I was reading the letters.

I expect you have wondered why I had not answered your letter & "budders" before now. I was in Sumpter eating sugar cane.

The weather has been unseasonably warm until today. As an evidence of the warmth of the weather, I eat a fine watermelon on my birthday, which was Monday the 5th of the month. I found it in riding over a corn field where the negroes were gathering the corn crop. . . .

The crop of sugarcane in Sumpter is fine. The negroes have large patches all around their houses & every day some of the little ones would come to the house lugging a big cane as a present for me.

They will cut their cane after frost & then old man Jerry will go to grinding it in the little mill & boil it into syrup in the large boiler. Some of them expect to make a little sugar also. They have to plant the cane close to their houses, as the negroes in the neighborhood raise no cane, and if theirs was distant from the houses, it would be stolen. The young "darkies" made a great many enquiries about their young masters. Each one has selected you, budder or Howell as his master & wanted to send sugar cane ground peas & potatoes to you all, but my buggy was not large enough.

Mary Ann Cobb to Howell Cobb

Athens, December 7, 1849

Sylvia arose with an attack of Rheumatism, and tho she managed to get her breakfast put on the fire, when I went out I found her sitting upon a stool, leaning upon a stick, almost given out. After breakfast she was so unwell she had to return from the kitchen, and I placed Aggy in her stead to get dinner. Rachel cooked the other meals. . . .

Aunt Phillis is very bad off, and Sylvias attack has been equal in severity to the first in the summer. She kept out this morning and got breakfast with some assistance from Rachel. I found her at her biscuit tray, kneading the dough, when I went out.

Mary Ann Cobb to Howell Cobb

Athens, December 13, 1849

Having disposed of breakfast things, after unusual labor on my part, Aggy being sick and unable to attend to the dining room, I had to content myself with Sabina's services. . . .

Rachel wants to go to Milledgeville at Christmas, what do you say to it. I want your opinion. It will be inconvenient in my present situation, but it would only be a week.

Mary Ann Cobb to Howell Cobb

Athens, December 20, 1849

I have not engaged a place for Polly, but I have an advertisement in the papers. Aggy's health failed so much after you left that I sent her to Dr. Moore, and requested him to consider her as one of his patients until she was restored to health. She and Sylvia take it by turn to be up, and I have decided that it will be too great a demand upon my patience and comfort to allow Rachel to leave here at Christmas, and in consequence I shall tell her to make herself contented, and if Bob [Cole] is to be the cause of her annoying me, he can return as soon as she wishes.

Ought I to furnish him with clothes? Wilkes took him as an apprentice, and I do not know the rules common in such matters.[45]

Mary Ann Cobb to Howell Cobb

Athens, December 24, 1849

I could not let Rachel go to Milledgeville. Sylvia & Aggy are too often sick for me to depend upon either in Rachels absence. I shall be obliged to let Jim off, and I shall be bothered the whole time he is gone.

William W. Birtle to Howell Cobb

[location unknown], January 23, 1850

A most unpleasant occurrence has just thrown our family into a painfully agitated state, and as their protector I feel bound to make it known to you, as I doubt not you will promptly apply the proper remedy to prevent its recurrence.

Your servant man Jackson has been for several nights suspected of introducing a strumpet into our house, and to night I found her in his room. Such an occurrence has never before come to our knowledge, and in order to secure us from a repetition of it, I ask his dismissal.

Having punished her, I have notified him of my intention to inform you, & told him that he must leave the house.

---

45. Wilkes Flagg had taken his nephew, the son of Rachel and Coleman Cole, to Milledgeville to train as a blacksmith.

Mary Ann Cobb to Howell Cobb

Athens, March 15, 1850

Your letter of the 10th came by yesterdays mail and I am obliged to you for your suggestions about servants. . . .

This morning I find that [Rachel's] babe weaned herself some weeks since, owing to the fact that she got no nourishment. . . .

The child is very delicate, and altho' now in her fifteenth month has only two teeth, which will throw her teething season into this summer, and I will have to give up the idea of taking Rachel with me, for should anything happen to her child during her absence, I should probably blame myself in a great measure.

Mary Ann Cobb to Howell Cobb

Athens, March 26, 1850

I have decided to take Eliza & Aggy [to Washington, D.C.]. Rachel was willing to go if I would take the whole responsibility of taking her from her children, and esteem the sacrifice a great favor to me. Brother John and I concluded that it would be best to take Eliza, as the other arrangement wished more trouble from the fact that my old mammy[46] would have to be brought from Milledgeville to take care of the children, and that would of course be a sacrifice to her and another favor to me.

Eliza is well disposed, honest & truthful, and desirous [to] please me even to excess causing awkwardness frequently and by proper care & training she will make a capital nurse. . . .

Howell Cobb to Mary Ann Cobb

Washington, D.C., April 6, 1850

I am not quite certain that I understand what disposition you have determined to make of the servants during your absence. They ought certainly be able to support themselves if left to appropriate their own time

---

46. Rachel's mother, Jenny Lamar.

to themselves. . . . In reference to Rachel it is different, as *her situation* may render her incapable of doing any thing for herself during a great part of the time. Upon the whole I would give them partial allowances and should they from sickness or other cause need more it would be convenient to arrange for such a contingency through John [B. Cobb] at any time.

Mary Ann Cobb to Howell Cobb
Athens, [1850]

Before you left for Habersham you told James to look out for some man to cut wood. . . . If you say so we will try and get George Carter. Poor fellow he is crazy to come home as he calls it. But it will be a poor speculation to buy an old negro when we can pick out a half dozen young ones at the plantation.

Mary Ann Cobb to John B. Lamar
Athens, December 30, 1853

Poor Bob only survived until 7 o'clock on saturday morning the 24th inst. It was a terrible day, snow falling heavily about two o'clock in the afternoon. I suffered much in mind and body that day, and but for the timely assistance of Coleman, I do not know what I would have done. . . . We have had a dreary christmas, the weather being cold and rainy, a scarcity of wood, no servants to wait upon us.

John Newton and William Wood[47] to Howell Cobb
Athens, December 1853

December	12	1 small pine table for office	$1.50
	24	1 coffin for servant	$5.00

---

47. William Wood was a cabinetmaker who made and sold furniture and coffins through Newton's general store in downtown Athens.

Sarah Prince to Mary Ann Cobb

Moreton Hampstead, January 6, 1854

We were shocked to hear of Uncle Bob's death. Poor old man! there are not many recollections of my past life in which his form is not conspicuously presented to my mind's eye. . . . Gradually are the old in our connexion (white & colored) departing for those unknown shores, where they can be followed no more by "mortal ken." This reflection necessarily brings sadness with it, but it need not produce gloom. How blessed the thought there is a *Power* who can lead us to realize *He* has taken from the grave "all its darkness & gloom."

Mary Ann Cobb to John B. Lamar

Athens, April 10, 1854

Mrs. Thomas' mortgage[48] [covers] Sylvia and her two daughters, and the increasing value of the latter inclines me to take every necessary precaution to secure them to myself and my children, I have taken a great deal of pains with them, and I am beginning to reap the benefit of my care and training for they are now a daily source of comfort to me in every kind of work I put them to, and they are so capable that they learn readily all that is taught them. Polly is getting to be an excellent washer and ironer, cook, and gardener, and Eliza is a neat house servant, washer and ironer, and sews well, and has some knowledge of cooking.

It is my desire to secure Eliza for Mary Ann as she nursed her, and she is so amiable and trustworthy.

Polly I wish also secured in some way, so that both of them shall decend to my children and their children. For it will be cruel if after all my trouble with them, that they should pass into strangers hands. Will you have this matter in mind, and when this mortgage is preclosed, have them and their mother settled upon me and my children. The mortgage will be

---

48. Mrs. Peninah Thomas, who had purchased the Cobbs' Pope Street house following Howell's bankruptcy in 1843, held a mortgage on Sylvia and her children. While the date of the mortgage is unclear, it seems likely that it was executed in 1843 and was the mechanism by which the Cobbs retained possession of the family.

paid off with the proceeds of the plantation, and I will have a right to ask this favor of Mr. Cobb, particularly as the negroes will go to his children.

You know you would miss Louisa and Uncle Davy, and if you had trained them yourself, you would then realize my fears and feelings upon the present subject, were you threatened with the loss of them. Past experience teaches me the necessity of looking ahead and preventing that which threatens the hold we have upon property.

Mary Ann Cobb to John B. Lamar

Athens, November 12, 1854

I have a request to make of you. Beck has a fine girl child, which has no nurse and it is carried to Charity to take care of it. As she was unfortunate with her first, her mother, my old nurse [Jenny Lamar] thinks she can do a better part by it than Beck can, and she wants to take it and raise.[49] I think it a good idea, and as it has *no father*, such children never fare well with their negro mothers. I think it will be better off with its grandmother. You will oblige me by agreeing to this arrangement. If you do, please write to Collins to let the old woman have the child.

Mary Ann Cobb to Howell Cobb

Athens, June 4, 1855

Rachel brought me a letter to read which she received from her Mother [Jenny Lamar] recently, and Howell could not read it for her. (It was miserably written and worse spelled.) I was really provoked beyond endurance with the old woman. She writes to Rachel sympathizing with her about being *separated* from her children, (as if they were thousands of miles off) and "not to *grieve* too much about them," and she hoped

---

49. It is worth noting that Jenny Lamar, located in Milledgeville, appears to have written a letter Mary Ann, in Athens, because she had heard via the network that her granddaughter on the Hurricane Plantation was receiving inadequate care. Mary Ann then wrote to her brother in Bibb County, asking him write to J. D. Collins, the overseer of Hurricane Plantation, to grant Jenny Lamar's request. N. C. Barnett's letter to John B. Lamar on October 4, 1860, indicates that John B. carried out his sister's wishes.

"no harm would befall them." The whole family are certainly the most ungrateful set that ever served indulgent owners. I wish they were *all* in Liberia. (I mean my old nurse & family.) I intend writing to the old woman and give her a plain talk, that will open her eyes, and sharpen her memory.

Charles F. McCay[50] to Howell Cobb

Columbia, South Carolina, October 8, 1855

I write to you about George. He has been talking to me to night about buying his son Nelson & expressed his anxiety to have some of his children with him when he gets old. I have thought it might be worth while to propose a sale of him to you. George is as faithful obedient industrious courteous & kind a servant as ever—his habits are as good as ever, tho' not perfect as he occasionally on Sundays drinks more than is good for him. His health is good. And he is in every respect satisfactory to us. He drives, hauls our wood, & makes our garden as he always did. . . .

I will sell for what you will say is a fair price. Please say if you will buy & how much you will give.

Charles F. McCay to Howell Cobb

Columbia, South Carolina, November 1, 1855

Two years ago I named $700 for George, but I have thought since it was a high price then. I believe if I remember rightly you offered $500. He is now older by this two years & that diminishes his value. Still as he can be hired for 12 or 15 dollars a month yet, he is still worth not a little. . . . George is so honest, so good-natured, so kind, so respectful that he can never cease to be valuable when he shall become old.

---

50. Charles F. McCay (March 8, 1810–March 13, 1889), a rigorous and unpopular former professor of mathematics at Franklin College, became a professor at South Carolina College and later president there. Augustus Longstreet Hull, *Annals of Athens, 1801–1901* (Athens: Banner Job Office, 1906), 186.

Mary Ann Cobb to Howell Cobb

Athens, November 6, 1855

A letter came last night from Mr McCay, which I enclose to you. It is a
wily article, a sample of the arch-Professor's cunning and duplicity. . . . I
would like to own George, but I am very *unwilling* that you shall be *swin-
dled* by McCay. . . . Be on your guard. He has reduced it to a mathematical
certainty that George is not worth $450. . . . Two years ago it *would have
been* a moderate price, but from the fact that McCay admits that George
has lost something in value in two years, I firmly believe that George is a
diseased negro, and Mr McCay *knows* he will in a few years have him upon
his hands—a helpless old man. . . . If my suspicion is correct, he judges
rightly in thinking doubtless—it will be to the advantage of George to be
owned by a *Southern born slave holder*—for only *such* knows how to bear pa-
tiently with the old age of negroes—and return to them in kindness and
care—full measure for their former years of service. I feel for George,
and if you were out of debt I would be willing that you should purchase
him, even if he could do no more than clean boots, that his old age might
be passed in the society of his children and with you and your children
to whom I know he is deeply attached. . . . I inquired of Aggy again about
her father, and she told me "a horse kicked him in the chest, and hurt
him badly, but he thought he was over all trouble with it, 'till one night
he awoke in the night nearly suffocated with blood coming from his
throat. . . ." Could you take George on trial? . . . If I were you I should
most assuredly let McCay know that you had heard of George's accident.
McCay never would have . . . brought his price from 700 to 450$ if he was
not convinced that George was not worth 450$.

Mary Ann Cobb to Howell Cobb

Athens, November 30, 1855

I send you some letters. Read Mr. McCay's and send it back that I may
file it away, for future use. Write me exactly what you want done in the
premises. I sent for Tom,[51] showed him the letter. . . . He then said he

---

51. Howell's younger brother, Thomas Reade Rootes Cobb (April 10, 1823–December
13, 1862).

would write to Mr. McCay and draw a bill of sale and . . . make McCay deliver George here at Christmas. . . . Do write me exactly how I ought to proceed.

Howell Cobb to Mary Ann Cobb

Washington, D.C., December 14, 1855

By this mornings mail I received your letter enclosing various letters, among others one from Mr McCay. I have this moment replied to him, saying that if he would send George to Tom at Athens at Christmas, that the money would be paid to him.

Thomas Reade Rootes Cobb to Mary Ann Cobb

Athens, January 3, 1856

Your covering check for $300, is received. As I may be absent when George comes I have turned over the check to John Cobb & have written again to Mr. McCay that the money is ready for him, on delivery of the boy.[52] I will see that the Bill of Sale is taken properly.

Mary Ann Cobb to Howell Cobb

Athens, January 11, 1856

I wrote to Tom to day, saying that "I was unwilling to take George in his present condition, and I would not consent to take him at any price without a warranty". . . . You remember the *cause* which prevented George's going with us to Ala in 1839. I suspect the same *disease* has returned upon him. If so, in his old age it will cripple if not destroy him completely. I would have liked to own George as he was in '/53, but I cannot say truthfully that I want him in an unsound condition. We are not in a situation to buy negroes purely from humanity. If any body is to suffer from George's infirm old age Mr. McCay is the man, because George has paid

52. "John Cobb" refers to Howell and Thomas's younger brother, John Boswell Cobb (February 3, 1826–November 21, 1893).

his original price more than 4 times in hire since 1840. Mr. McCay has got out [of] him more than we would have in 20 years.

I have brought myself I think to the proper point, with Rachel, *I want to part with her*. Shall I give her an opportunity to get a master if she can? or shall I send her to the plantation without such a preliminary? Let me know at once which plan you approve. My plan is to send her down the last of the winter or the beginning of Spring. I have borne with her for 23 years, and that is far enough. I cannot endure the idea of going through life with such an incubus, as she and her family have become by their worthlessness and insolence.

Mary Ann Cobb to Howell Cobb

Athens, January 17, 1856

Poor George. I fear me his complaint is worse than Rheumatism. I could stand a Rheumatic negro, but the other disease would make the victim loathsome, more and more the longer he lives, and besides I would have to give up Aggy entirely to attend to him. It would be ruinous to my comfort and peace of mind to carry the project any further. He has made money enough for McCay to entitle him to a decent support the remainder of his life, and he can show now whether he is an adopted son of the South in heart and in principle, by taking care of his old negro. When McCay made the first offer to you, he knew in his heart that George was worthless. . . . Send me back McCays letter. I wish to preserve it.

Howell Cobb to Mary Ann Cobb

Washington, D.C., January 17, 1856

In reference to the purchase of George, I am much at a loss what to say or do. . . . I know your feelings about this matter and sympathizing with you, in the whole affair, in your desire to gratify both George & Aggy.

Mary Ann Cobb to Howell Cobb

Athens, January 31, 1856

I have been waiting anxiously for a reply from you in reference to Rachel and her family. Something must be done. I do not believe I can ever have confidence in her honesty or affection for me, and I cannot live longer with one who has lost my confidence so irrevocably as she has. I wish to know of you, if you think it best to give her a permit to look for a master. If you think this unnecessary kindness to her in consideration of her ingratitude and uniform disrespect and disobedience to my commands. She will then be sent to the plantation in the Spring. The character of her husband is another strong inducement to get rid of her.

Jenny Lamar to Mary Ann Cobb

Milledgeville, September 29, 1856

Dear Mistress

I am somewhat loth to make the request I want if you can . . . buy my husband [Bob]. He is old . . . and will be of verry little service to you but he is my husband and I do not want to be parted from him. Mr Perry is going to move to Alabama. Dear Mistress this is a great deal to ask of you but I have no one to go to but you. I am tolerable well at present making out to live through these hard times. Give my love to all the children and Master and receive a great deal for yourself and to mars Andrew children also and to Rachel and her children. I have nothing more to say at present but remain your humble servant.

Jenny Lamar

Charles F. McCay to Howell Cobb

Columbia, South Carolina, January 13, 1857

Our servants have boxed up at the request of your Aggy the bed and clothes left by our old man George & sent them to day to the Rail Road directed to your care.

Hoping they will reach her safely.

Henry Darby[53] to John B. Lamar

Macon, May 28, 1857

Dear Master,

The *mares* have both refused the horse and Mr. Mason think that they are both with fold [foal]. I was at the Plantation yesterday drilling rock for Mr. Rose to put the Ink into. He has got all the gin house weatherboarded but one side and said he would finish it in a few weeks. Mr. Lovi is going out monday to commence painting. He will finish the painting here in about ten days. The crops have improved very much since you left and they look much better that you would expect them at this time. Your garden looks very fine considering, and all the trees are all *dead* and but 2 living. The one at the corner of the office and the other end of the house, both in front of the house are *dead*. I am going to sumter tomorrow as Mr. Mason think the mares can travel. Old Hall's mare has improved very much since you left and I think she is with fold too.

From Your Humble servant
Henry Darby

Mary Ann Cobb to Howell Cobb

Athens, June 17, 1857

Rachel is quite expert at "upholstering." I have had only to make suggestions to her, and she executes them to my satisfaction . . . she is by far the smartest negro we have, and if *she* only possessed Sylvia or Aggys disposition I would not leave Georgia without her. She has served me faithfully and cheerfully for three months past, and it grieves me to remember that an overseer has to lord it over her for the next few years. She is too smart a negro to be on [a] plantation. I am unfit to deal with negroes . . . faithful service or the slightest evidence of repentance . . . on their part banishes all my hard feelings—and *years* of insubordination—and insolence are forgotten.

---

53. John B. Lamar's body servant. Prior to serving in Lamar's house in Macon, Darby was enslaved on one of the Sumter County plantations. Henry was most likely the son of Jim Darby, who, with his wife and children, had been relocated to Sumter County around 1848.

John A. Cobb II to Mary Ann Cobb

Athens, September 29, 1857

Coleman has been after me to know what was to be done with Rachel & her family. I told him that if she was hired out it would be impossible for her to keep but two of her children and that the rest would [have] to go to the plantation [at] Christmas.

Jenny Lamar to John B. Lamar

Milledgeville, March 21, 1858

My Deare Master

I know you will be surprised at receiving a letter from me, but When I tell you why I do write I hope you will forgive me. I have just returned from the plantation where I have been to see My Daughter Becky. She has bine Confined. She gave birth to two Children.[54] She is now very sick indeed and I know that when here time is out the overseere will have here out at work wich is not right for she will have enough to do you know my Master to tend to them two Children. This is why I write. It is all about here and for here and I wish you my kind Master to have some way fixed that she may take care of them if you will. I now God will bless you for it that she may either stay and tend to them here self or that some of the rest may tend to them for the overseere I know is cruel to them for he is starving some of them by not giving them enough to eate. This I now for I now I would not write that I did not know and if you do not have some way fixed so that she may take care of them she will go to work two soon and not only will the children suffer but she will die hereself. So my Good Master have pitty on here for God sake and have something done and I wish you would be so Good to send me some money to have here

54. Becky appears to have given birth to twins. One of these was named Alan Lamar, but there is no record of the name given to his sibling. Jenny Lamar had been successful in petitioning Mary Ann to protect Becky's newborn "fine girl child" in 1854, as the infant was ultimately placed in her care. It is worth noting that she wrote here to John B. instead, as Mary Ann had clearly taken umbrage at learning of her 1855 letters to Rachel about the location and well-being of Rachel's children.

children some clothes made or send me some flannel or something to make them. Do this My Kind Master and I know God will bless you.

Jinny Lamar

Do answer this my kind Master as soon as you get it and forgive me for troubling you with a line but I do hope you will do something for my Child becky.

Jinny Lamar

John B. Lamar to Mary Ann Cobb
Macon, June 12, 1858

Alfred is at the Sumter plantation. I will send Rachel to the Hurricane this fall.

John A. Cobb II to Mary Ann Cobb
Athens, August 9, 1858

Rachels family left here for the plantation on Saturday morning. She went off very quietly. I sent all except [her children] Bob Lawrence & Lucius. Lawrence is hired out. Bob I wanted to take care of my horse & Lucius is sick with his old complaint and & Dr Long told me if he staid here that he could cure him.

Mary Ann Cobb to John A. Cobb II
Washington, D.C., August 20, 1858

Your letters have been received. The last one dated the 9th of this month, occasioned me some pain. I had no thought of your sending Rachel to the plantation before Oct. or Nov. You did not tell me you had any such intention, or I should have opposed it. After so long a residence in a high and healthy latitude, it is extremely hazardous to send the family off to Baldwin in the middle of the sickly season there and in all bilious climates. The only way I can acct for this sudden and extraordinary step, is that you and your Uncle agreed upon it, whilst you were here, but as it

was a matter of my own, you should have at least mentioned it to me. Another thing I regret is that you did not send Bob with his Mother that she
might have had him to assist her in her new home. As it is, tending your
horse 'till Christmas will keep him the greater part of the time in a state
of idleness leading the way to his falling into bad company and contract-
ing bad habits. I would rather see you cultivate a feeling of kind consideration for all who are dependent upon you, than to observe as I do *painfully* that it is your desire to be arbitrary and merciless, forgetting that
God looks into the heart, and knows our inmost thoughts, and intentions, and he will show mercy unto those who are *merciful,* but will plint-
ifully reward the wicked doer. It is wicked to be unkind and inconsider-
ate toward the feelings of others, especially to those who are dependent
upon us and completely in our power. . . . It is my wish that Bob shall go
to the plantation at Christmas. I wish you to remember this and if my *wish*
is not carried out, I shall consider myself treated with great disrespect, of
which I trust my son is incapable towards his mother. Lucius' case is different. If he can be cured, it is better he should remain in Athens where
he can be more regularly attended than on a plantation. . . . How did
Rachel go? Is the plantation wagon a hired wagon. Did she take all her
things? If not, when is she to get the remainder? After she gets her things
away, I would suggest one thing, that you have her house locked up and
the key put into the *work stand.* If you do not Coleman will keep his residence there, and there's no telling the amount of unlawful gatherings,
and [no] work will be carried on there.

Easter to Her "Dear Father"

Athens, June 27, 1859

I staid with your Mother two weeks and two days. I also staid Two weeks
and two days in Macon. When I left your Mother she was well and harty
and all your brothers and sisters sent their love to you. I have been well
ever since I have been up here and my baby too.[55] Your Mother says if she
never sees you again she wants to meet you in heaven. I and the baby are
getting along as well as you could expect. I want to do the same as your

---

55. Easter was moved to Athens from the Hurricane Plantation to serve as a wet nurse for
a local family. See Mary Ann Cobb to Howell Cobb, June 27, 1859.

Mother said if I never see you again I want to meet you in heaven. All
your friends send you their love. Give all my love to my husband. Remember my love to all my sisters and brothers and likewise to my Uncles and
Aunts and Cousins too. Tell my husband that I still hold on to what I was
then. I went to uncle ben Robinsons and staid a half of a day. He and his
wife both sent their love to you. There was no one dead [at] Baldwin but
there was one lying at the point of death when I left. You must write to me
soon. I staid with your Mother all the time except one night and then I
staid with your brother that night. Good by dear Father.

Your affectionate daughter,

Easter

Lamar Cobb to Mary Ann Cobb
Athens, January 11, 1860

You ask me about the negroes, all are well. Lucius is getting along pretty
well. I promised him he should go to see his mother Christmas with his
father. But Coleman was taken sick & did not go. Yesterday his Uncle Wilkes Flag came & told him he would carry him down & pay his expenses if
I would let him go. I gave him a pass & told him to go. Also a note to the
overseer telling him to send him back by Coleman when he goes down
next time. Coleman will go down perhaps next week & Lucius is to come
back with him. All the rest are well. Polly I have hired to Mr. Scudder for
the rest of this month. I have been unable to hire her as yet but expect
Mr. Scudder will take her the rest of the year. I thought it better to hire
her for the rest of the month than have her running about town working
for twenty five cents a day or doing nothing.

N. C. Barnett[56] to John B. Lamar

Milledgeville, October 4, 1860

I have been instructed by the Mayor of this City, to inform you, that you have one or two negro slaves living here in violation of the Laws and ordinances of the City; and that they must be removed or placed on the premises and under the control and oversight of some responsible white person.

The name of one of the negroes, he informs me, is Jenny, the other, a young girl, name not known to the Mayor, but living in the house with old Jenny.

His Honor has directed me to cite you to the act, which you will find at "Page 223, Pamphlet acts of 1831."[57]

Mary Ann Cobb to Howell Cobb

Athens, October 2, 1863

Eliza is all hands on busy making cake & cleaning up, for her wedding on Tuesday.

---

56. Nathan Crawford Barnett (June 28, 1801–February 3, 1890) served as the Georgia secretary of state (1843–49, 1851–53, 1861–68) and the clerk of the City of Milledgeville. For the strict limits the State of Georgia placed upon free black people, as well as free-living enslaved people like Jenny Lamar (the subject of this letter), see Tera W. Hunter, *Bound in Wedlock: Slave and Free Black Marriage in the Nineteenth Century* (Cambridge: Belknap Press of Harvard University Press, 2017), 87, 102–3.

57. State law prohibited the enslaved from hiring their own time "or to live upon a lot separate and apart from his or her owner or manager." It further prevented white owners from hiring those they enslaved to anyone with the intent of allowing them to live independently. Enslaved people caught violating the law faced imprisonment in county jail until their owner paid their jail fees. *Acts of the General Assembly of the State of Georgia, Passed in Milledgeville at an Annual Session in November and December, 1831* (Milledgeville, Ga.: Prince & Ragland, 1832), 223–24.

Mary Ann Cobb to Howell Cobb

Athens, [October 1863]

Eliza's marriage will not take place next tuesday as was expected. Howard
Jones came up last night and brought a letter he had received from Wm
De Lyons' wife in Savh. claiming him as her lawful husband, and Howard
is opposed to the match. Eliza yields to her brother's better judgement
but thinks he has been very dilatory in his opposition, which I think too.
He disclaims all intention to break off the match but merely wished to lay
the facts before Eliza and let her decide for herself. Eliza is hurt with him.
The children had given her money enough to buy a bridal hat, and I had
given her from thursday 'til tuesday to make her cake & other preparations. I gave her flour, butter, lard, and . . . a few pounds of white sugar
for icing her cake. She and Polly & Melinda baked all the cake, and Vicey
baked 4 large pones of Light bread yesterday, and I liked to have had the
hams boiled yesterday for expedition. I intended giving her two hams
and a Turkey. My kitchen was cleaned out yesterday for the supper room,
the whole yard nicely swept, and the middle of last week our cottage parlor was scoured and emptied of Howell's furniture preparatory to be used
as a reception room for Eliza's guests. Mr Ivy was to have performed the
ceremony, but Howard has knocked everything into a pie. I told Eliza not
to mind it, "there was as good fish in the sea as one was caught out," better luck next time, to pack up her finery and "bide her time." She tried at
first to bear it cheerfully, but it goes hard with her.

To save William unnecessary mortification, I have suggested to Howard
to go to Union Point tomorrow, meet him and tell him of Eliza's decision
and give him and his mother & his friends an opportunity to go quietly
to Augusta by the return train. He will leave in the morning and I will de-
fray his expenses. This arrangement will save Eliza an unpleasant meeting with William. Throughout this untoward affair I have left her to act
as she pleased though it was not a desirable arrangement for me. I would
have prefered her taking some man nearer home whom she knew something about. Never having seen any good come of interference on the
part of owners in their servants matrimonial arrangements I am determined Eliza should have no cause for cursing me in future for her leading a worse life.

Mary Ann Cobb to Howell Cobb

Athens, October 8, 1863

De Lyons has come in tonight and showed me a letter . . . from his former wife, in which she disclaims writing the letter Howard brought . . . Eliza has had an interview with her love and says, "she is satisfied," and is willing to "take him for better or for worse." I have told De L, he must bring that letter he said his master had written, before I could consent. He will leave for Augusta tomorrow.

Mary Ann Cobb to Howell Cobb

Athens, October 18, 1863

Today I gave notice to Aggy that there ought to be a dinner for the bride & groom. A table was set with my crockery etc and I guess the colored folks had a good time. I let Eliza have the old parlor (cottage) to receive her company in today. Her supper table was set in it last night. Everything was conducted . . . *elegantly*. Eliza has not forsaken the children. I released her from her duties, but she . . . came in this morning to dress them and again to put them to bed. The children do not relish her marrying. Lizzie says she wants Mr. DeLyons to quit Eliza, and go back home. This morning Andrew & Lizzie had a thousand and one questions to ask Eliza finally Andrew said Eliza why did'nt you tell Mr. De Lyons you didnt want to marry, before Eliza could reply Lizzie put in her voice "Because you would be telling a big story wouldn't *you Eliza?*" She asked Eliza who married you. Eliza said Mr. Ivy.[58] At this she laughed so heartily I rather inferred she thought Mr. Ivy was the bridegroom.

---

58. Revered F. H. Ivey was pastor of Athens's First Baptist Church.

Mary Ann Cobb to Howell Cobb

Athens, October 25, 1863

Howell [Jr.] tells me Mr. Whitner[59] asked him "what sort of negro Polly was?" and he must have made the impression upon Mr. W's mind by what he said that we wanted to get rid of her. You ought to correct this . . . . She is in good health now, has been washing for me for two months, gives perfect satisfaction, and seems determined to try to please me & do her duty in every respect. I have had to change her from one kind of work to another of late, and have had no cause of complaint. She is capable of doing anything well. My course of treatment to her last spring seems to have effected a change in her as far as I am concerned, and had I to depend on only one or two servants I would not ask for a better hand for all work than Polly, but she would do better on a lot alone or with few negroes, as her disposition is to be head maid and when she comes in contact with one of her own head a fuss is likely to take place, there has been none here, since her confinement, for I made her understand that was meddling with my prerogative. . . . She is a little lame, but . . . when Eliza was married she was as active as a kitten, cleaning up & scouring baking cake & dressing herself & the girls for the wedding. . . . My head is so confused. But please help me in having Polly removed from our lot.

59. John Charles Whitner (September 23, 1831–January 15, 1906) was married to Howell's sister, Sarah Martha Cobb.

Lithograph of Mary Ann Cobb, ca. 1850s.
Courtesy of Deborah Kehaulani Young Leathers.

Howell Cobb, ca. 1850s.
Courtesy of the Library of Congress.

John B. Lamar, ca. 1850s.
Courtesy of Hargrett Rare Book and Manuscript Library,
University of Georgia Libraries.

An enslaved woman in Athens, Georgia, 1858. There were few families
in Athens who could afford to, or were willing to, have a portrait
made of an enslaved person. Given those circumstances, as well as
the inclusion of a book suggesting this woman's literacy, it is highly
improbable that it could be anyone other than Aggy Mills.
Courtesy of Georgia Archives, Vanishing Georgia Collection, clr210–92.

Cowpens Plantation House, Walton County, Georgia, 1938.
Photograph by Julia Cook Brackett, courtesy of Benjamin G. Brackett.

Howell and Mary Ann Cobb's first home,
Pope Street, Athens, Georgia, 2013.
Courtesy of the Peterson family.

John B. Lamar's home, the "Bear's Den," Walnut Street,
Macon, Georgia, 1936. *Courtesy of the Library of Congress.*

Georgia,
Clarke County.

WHEREAS, by virtue of a writ of Fieri Facias, to me directed, from the Honorable *Superior Court of said County* —————— wher *H. S.* of the *State of Georgia* —————— *was* p—————— *Cobb Indent* —————— *was* defendant et——— levy on *a* certain *Negro girl named Aggy about Seven* *Years of age.*

which said *Negro Girl* being by me advertised according to law, was, on the day of the *Fourth October Instant* exposed to public sale and outcry, at the *house of Howell Cobb in the town of Athens* in satisfaction of the said Execution, when *John B. Lamar* being the highest bidder, the said *Negro Child* was knocked off to him for the sum of *Four hundred.* —————— Dollars:

Now therefore, I, *James Hendon* —————— Sheriff of the *County* —————— aforesaid, for and in consideration of the sum of *four hundred.* —————— Dollars, to me in hand paid by th——— said *John P. Lamar* — the receipt whereof is hereby ledged, have bargained, sold and delivered, and by these presents do barg—— the said *John P. Lamar* — the said *Neg* which said *Negro Girl* I do warrant and defend unto the said *John Lamar* — his heirs and assigns forever, as far as by law a Sheriff is bound warrant and defend in such case.

In witness whereof, I have hereunto set my hand and seal, this *twenty first* day of *October* —————— 1843 ,

Three erasures and two interlineations made before signed

Henry Hull
S. L. Mays Not Public

James Hendon Sheriff.

October 1843 bill of sale for "a certain negro girl named Aggy about Seventeen Years of age. . . ." According to the document, she was auctioned in front of the Cobbs' Pope Street house ("when John B. Lamar being the highest bidder, the said Negro Girl was knocked off to him for the sum of four hundred Dollars").
Courtesy of Hargrett Rare Book and Manuscript Library, University of Georgia Libraries.

4th march the

my dear little sister

I have ben wanting to rite to you for sum time
but I could not rite as I had one of my eys bad by
hurt that for I hope you will not think that I am
no gratful to you and my dear sister for the nice
and hand sun presants theat she sent to me and my
childearn I do wish that it was in my power to
rite how gratful and thankful I am to you and
I hope the Lord will spar me long or nuf to rase
my children to feel the same ____ ____ me in my
thanks to you and ____ ____ ____ the member
dusty I am trooly glad to have that yer all will
be home this ____ ____ how happy I will be to see
your dear little ____ a gun and more then happy
to see the little ____ ____ is rrany yer to I want
to see her dear little ____ ____ nuch ended
the trees and flowers ar puting out very pritty
near + now but we have a gread del of rane
nirs mill ____ ____ har got very well a gune
nirs kar ____ har a fine sun and nirs ____ Ma has
a fine darter all doning very well that is
all of the ____ that I ____ ____ will at ____ to

March 1857 letter from Aggy Mills to the Cobb children. Aggy explains that an eye injury kept her from writing sooner, adding, "I hope you will not think that I am ungratful to you. . . . Oh I do wish it was in my power to rite how gratful and thankful I am to you and I hope the lord well spar me long ornuf to rase my childran to feel the same. Lu [joins] me in menny thanks to you and frances wod too if she new her duty." Importantly, she concludes by noting, "I hope you well excuse my spellig as thar is grat meny mestaks."

Courtesy of Hargrett Rare Book and Manuscript Library,
University of Georgia Libraries.

March 1865 letter from Aggy Mills to Mary Ann Cobb, who had fled to
Americus to avoid General W. T. Sherman's approach to Athens. With a
clear hand and refined language, Aggy wrote that she was "very glad to hear
that you are coming home this summer. We all wish to see you very much.
I am planting both gardens and if you have any particular directions to send
you can let me know as I have just commenced planting." Mary Ann saw
Aggy's improved writing skills as evidence of duplicity.

Courtesy of Hargrett Rare Book and Manuscript
Library, University of Georgia Libraries.

CHAPTER 3

"Everything Is Deranged about the House . . . There Is No Head or Foot, No Mistress or Maid"

THE ENSLAVED SURVIVED IN AN UNJUST and brutal world. They had limited capacity to protect themselves or their families from the actions of those who held power over them, an owner's sudden death, or even the vicissitudes of the national economy. Most possessed no real alternative to performing the roles demanded by the existing system, however much they might dislike the necessity. They certainly resented this vulnerability. Yet, simultaneously, those enslaved by the Cobb-Lamar family knew they had the means to shape their immediate situations and frequently tried to do so. For example, field hands on the family's plantations negotiated the right to supplement the monotonous rations of corn and pork they received by growing watermelons and pumpkins, trapping wild turkeys, and raising sugar cane and selling the syrup. This cash, combined with money earned from a portion of the cotton crop, enabled them to secure additional items such as chickens, tobacco, extra clothing, and even alcohol.[1] They also understood that they had to work within the boundaries

---

1. The Cobb-Lamars designated a small percentage of their acreage for the financial profit of their enslaved workers. Discussions of selling sugar cane syrup and what they termed "the negro cotton" appear in numerous letters and receipts. See, for example, B. J. Brantley to John B. Lamar, February 23, 1842, Cobb-Erwin-Lamar Family Collection; John B. Lamar to John A. Cobb II, November 9, 1849; John B. Lamar to Mary Ann Lamar Cobb, January 13, 1859; Nathan Barwick to John B. Lamar, March 14, 1862; and the receipt for cotton weights dated August 31, 1842. See also Kathleen M. Hilliard, *Masters, Slaves, and Exchange: Power's Purchase in the Old South* (New York: Cambridge University Press, 2014), 155–57; Watson W. Jennison, *Cultivating Race: The Expansion of Slavery in Georgia, 1750–1860* (Lexington: University Press of Kentucky, 2012), 47; Susan O'Donovan, *Becoming Free in the Cotton South* (Cambridge: Harvard University Press, 2009), 41; Anthony E. Kaye, *Joining Places: Slave Neighborhoods of the Old South* (Chapel Hill: University of North Carolina Press, 2007), 105; Dylan C. Penningroth, *The Claims of Kinfolk: African American Property and Community in the Nineteenth-Century South* (Chapel Hill: University of North Carolina Press, 2003), 52–63; John Campbell, "As a 'Kind of Freeman'? Slaves' Market-Related Activities in South

negotiated with their enslavers over generations. In exchange for food, clothing, shelter, protection from physical abuse, and the ability to live in relatively close proximity to their families and kinship networks, most do not appear to have worked actively to undermine the system. Still, when the enslaved believed the Cobb-Lamars or their overseers acted counter to this unspoken agreement, resistance followed.[2]

The range of resistance—both open and subtle—proved highly complex. Those enslaved on the family's plantations and in their homes saw manipulation as the safest form of pushing back against violations of unspoken but long-negotiated agreements. The extent to which Aggy, Sylvia, or even Rachel succeeded or failed in their machinations likely resulted from their proximity to the Cobb-Lamars. Years of learning the culture of the household and the idiosyncrasies of the family enabled them to refine the forms and tones of resistance they employed. Yet the enslaved who came into the family homes from time on the plantation, whether they worked as skilled labor or field hands, often did not know these fine points of negotiation with masters they had less frequently encountered. For those in this liminal space between worlds, not yet fluent in household culture, reactions to transgressions of negotiated boundaries often lacked the subtlety of more seasoned household servants.[3]

Those who labored in the households had to learn to navigate a labyrinthine circumstance in which their owners, as a perquisite of their wealth, resolved conflicts by simply banishing those they deemed troublesome to far-off plantations. For the hundreds of people held on the plantations, however, banishment was not an option. There, the subtleties of psychological threat gave way to a system dictated by brute force.

The generations of the Cobb-Lamar family understood and accepted this harsh reality but attempted to moderate its worst aspects. They frequently voiced a desire to be humane but also needed to secure the acquiescence of their chattels in order for the system to function. Zachariah Lamar had often stipulated in overseer contracts that his overseers

Carolina," in *The Slaves' Economy: Independent Production by Slaves in the Americas,* ed. Ira Berlin and Phillip D. Morgan (New York: Routledge, 1991), 136–37.

2. Kelly Houston Jones, "'A Rough, Saucy Set of Hands to Manage': Slave Resistance in Arkansas," *Arkansas Historical Quarterly* 71, no. 1 (Spring 2012): 7–12; Peter Kolchin, *American Slavery, 1619–1877* (New York: Hill and Wang, 1993), 162–64; James Oakes, *Slavery and Freedom: An Interpretation of the Old South* (New York: W. W. Norton, 1990), 138–39; Paul D. Escott, *Slavery Remembered: A Record of Twentieth-Century Slave Narratives* (Chapel Hill: University of North Carolina Press, 1979), 78–79.

3. Escott, *Remembering Slavery,* 62.

must never engage in violence toward the enslaved that would result in their deaths or keep them from their "daily labor."[4] By the time his children inherited his estate, however, this caveat had been significantly modified to fit the needs of their growing business empire. Contracts after the mid-1830s required the overseers to employ physical punishment only in "moderation."[5] Zachariah had provided a clear delineation of when an overseer had exceeded his authority, but his heirs' stipulation of "moderation" left the definition of excessive punishment to be defined by the overseer and contested by the enslaved.

While the family could attempt to keep their hands clean by choosing not to grip the lash, their overseers did not possess that luxury. Rather, they found themselves caught between two masters. Their employers demanded both strict but reasonable regulation of the enslaved and an abundant crop of cotton, corn, and hogs, but overseers also supervised an involuntary workforce that resisted excessive work or punishment. Jonas Smith, an overseer fired from the family's Hurricane Plantation, complained that he could not "get on when the Imployer & negroes & avery boddy else" was against him.[6] As Smith's frustration suggests, those held on plantations demonstrated skills at resistance as adept as, but more overt than, those held within the household.

When those enslaved on one of the Sumter County plantations became dissatisfied with overseer Stancil Barwick's management, they secured aid from an anonymous writer to report their complaints to John B. Lamar. They accused Barwick of mismanaging hog production, excessively relying on the whip, and working some enslaved pregnant women to the point that they miscarried. "You have no ydea the cruel management them negroes has to under go," they warned, "I wonder they dont

---

4. Overseer contract between Zachariah Lamar and Henry Morris, September 3, 1831. See also overseer contract between Zachariah Lamar and Alexander Edge, September 3, 1831.

5. John B. Lamar to John Roberson, November 4, 1846.

6. Jonas Smith to John B. Lamar, July 22, 1852. Tristan Stubbs, *Masters of Violence: The Plantation Overseers of Eighteenth-Century Virginia, South Carolina, and Georgia* (Columbia: University of South Carolina Press, 2018). See also Kaye, *Joining Places*, 137, 140–41; Oakes, *Slavery and Freedom*, 21–22; Mark S, Shantz, "'A Very Serious Business': Managerial Relationships on the Ball Plantations," *South Carolina Historical Magazine* 88, no. 1 (January 1987): 1–22; J. William Harris, *Plain Folk and Gentry in a Slave Society: White Liberty and Black Slavery in Augusta's Hinterlands* (Baton Rouge: Louisiana State University Press, 1985), 90–93, 151–52; William Kauffman Scarborough, *The Overseer: Plantation Management in the Old South* (Baton Rouge: Louisiana State University Press, 1966).

all Run away."[7] They also shared their complaints with the plantation doctor. He reported them to John B., who immediately demanded an explanation from his overseer. Barwick acknowledged the two miscarriages but denied that either resulted from overwork. He also acknowledged that he had been compelled to resort to whipping "two or three hard cases," but he denied that he had ever behaved "cruelly."[8] John B. found Barwick's defense acceptable, but the simple act of his intervention also calmed the immediate situation. The overseer remained in the family's employ for more than a decade.

Not every conflict between overseers and the enslaved was resolved so easily. When a complaint failed to rectify their problem, the enslaved escalated their modes of resistance by breaking tools, false-packing cotton bales, abusing livestock, and simply refusing to work. By sabotaging the profitability of the plantation, they held the power to compel the Cobb-Lamars to heed their dissatisfaction. Sometimes even that was not sufficient. In February 1837 Mary Ann reported to Howell that people enslaved on the Hurricane Plantation had attempted to poison overseer Simon Ruff. Ruff faced a nearly chaotic situation at the Hurricane. He had pushed the plantation's labor force to the brink of outright rebellion by abusive physical punishments, wild threats against their lives, and, it was alleged, raping enslaved women.[9] The family was outraged but cast blame on everyone involved. Howell immediately fired the overseer, but

7. "A Friend" to John B. Lamar, June 6, 1855.

8. Stancil Barwick to John B. Lamar, July 13, 1855. Stancil Barwick (July 16, 1826–June 7, 1890) was an overseer at the Sumter County plantations. The Cobb children nicknamed him "Ransy Sniffle," based on the ugly, violent, and comical character in Augustus Baldwin Longstreet's *Georgia Scenes* (1840). Mary Ann and John B.'s cousin L. Q. C. Lamar, was married to Longstreet's daughter.

9. See David Doddington, "Manhood, Sex, and Power in Antebellum Slave Communities," in *Sexuality and Slavery: Reclaiming Intimate Histories in the Americas*, ed. Daina Ramey Berry and Leslie M. Harris (Athens: University of Georgia Press, 2018), 149–52; Tera W. Hunter, *Bound in Wedlock: Slave and Free Black Marriage in the Nineteenth Century* (Cambridge: Belknap Press of Harvard University Press, 2017), 32–33; Wilma King, "'Prematurely Knowing of Evil Things': The Sexual Abuse of African American Girls and Young Women in Slavery and Freedom," *Journal of African American History* 99, no. 3 (Summer 2014): 174–80; Daina Ramey Berry, *Swing the Sickle for the Harvest Is Ripe: Gender and Slavery in Antebellum Georgia* (Champaign: University of Illinois Press, 2007), 79, 100–103; Kaye, "Terrains of Struggle," chap. 4 in *Joining Places*; Stephanie M. H. Camp, *Closer to Freedom: Enslaved Women and Everyday Resistance in the Plantation South* (Chapel Hill: University of North Carolina Press, 2004), 50–51; Kolchin, *American Slavery*, 155–66; Drew Gilpin Faust, *James Henry Hammond and the Old South: A Design for Mastery* (Baton Rouge: Louisiana State University Press, 1982), 90–94; and Escott, *Slavery Remembered*, 86–90.

Mary Ann chided her husband, "[You will now] have to resort to some severe manner of treatment before you can compel [those enslaved at Hur-
ricane] to know their places. They are fully in the belief that they can do
as they please as everyone says that they have such a kind master."[10]

There is no evidence that the vast majority of people enslaved by the
family believed they could "do as they please," but they clearly developed
effective means of tempering the inclination of their overseers to act in
harsh or brutal ways. On the plantation, the existence of a hired overseer
often provided an additional level of negotiation and a scapegoat for conditions that satisfied neither owners nor the enslaved. For those forced to
make the transition from plantation to household service, the range of
options could narrow sharply. Those who failed to appreciate the difference between challenging the will of an overseer or employer and challenging their owner risked not only their place within the household but
also their presence in the larger community.

The potential hazards of miscalculation are especially clear in the story
of Alfred, the nineteen-year-old son of Abram and Hetty and grandson
of Levi. He had spent his life on the family's Sumter County plantations,
with his parents and multiple siblings, until John B. sent him to Athens in
1854. He thrived there for two years, apparently untroubled by the separation because, like so many of the people the Cobb-Lamars enslaved,
the vast network of connectivity allowed him to remain emotionally close
to his family despite the physical distance between them. It was only when
his owners broke what he believed was their unspoken agreement on unreasonable physical violence that Alfred instinctively resorted to the lessons he had learned over a lifetime in rural Sumter and ran. His act of
open resistance demonstrated his unfamiliarity with the subtle modes of
manipulation and protest developed by those experienced in the expectations of the household.

Alfred had worked as a "*regular waggoner*" on the Sumter County plantations and proven himself competent and reliable while delivering har-
vested cotton nearly thirty miles to the depot or traveling nearly eighty
miles to John B.'s home in Macon.[11] When Bob Scott died on Christmas
Eve, 1853, and after the family's mourning ended, John B. suggested that
they fill the hole left by the elderly servant's passing by moving up this

10. Mary Ann Cobb to Howell Cobb, February 1, 1837.
11. John B. Lamar to Mary Ann Cobb, January 5, 1854.

"lively, but steady chap." Mary Ann confessed that she did not know the
young man, but she had a favorable opinion of his grandparents and
therefore judged that he would make a suitable replacement.[12]

Alfred arrived in Athens late in 1854. For an ambitious young man,
there was great opportunity in assuming Bob's duties as a courier of
goods and a vital link in maintaining communications across the family's expansive holdings of land and people. He embraced this new life
and settled into the possibilities of the role. Mary Ann warmed to him as
well and declared, "I like very much the appearance and manners of my
new man Alfred"; she found him to be "a good match for his masters."[13]
Her evident appreciation—if not actual fondness—extended to the other
members of the family as well. When Howell and Mary Ann's oldest son,
John, traveled to Sumter County to pay the overseers their wages and to
distribute cotton money to the enslaved, Mary Ann noted that he carried
Alfred with him so that the young man might visit his mother. "And as
our boys are very thoughtful of Alfred's comfort," she continued, "I have
no doubt John has staid a day or two longer that Alfred may spend a portion of Christmas on the plantation."[14]

This satisfactory arrangement persisted for nearly two years. Then Alfred's world collapsed with an unexpected and abrupt act of brutality.
John B. had given Lamar Cobb, Howell and Mary Ann's second son,
an exquisite English-made saddle. The teenage Lamar was inordinately
proud of the gift and exploded in rage when he learned that Alfred had
loaned it without permission. His brother, John, described the incident
and its disastrous consequence. "Lamar whiped Alfred yesterday for lending out his saddle," he wrote to his uncle, "and in the evening when we
came home he could not be found and we have heard nothing of him
since, just at this time his absence puts everything out of place."[15]

Alfred expected that his absence following the beating would have
been seen by the Cobb-Lamars as a reasonable form of protest, as it would
have been understood on the plantation. They seem to have recognized
absenteeism, or "laying out," as a fair response following physical punishment by an overseer on a plantation.[16] When such behavior was directed

---

12. Ibid.

13. Mary Ann Cobb to John A. Cobb II, December 10, 1854.

14. Mary Ann Cobb to Howell Cobb, December 25, 1856.

15. John A. Cobb II to John B. Lamar, May 12, 1857.

16. See O'Donovan, *Becoming Free in the Cotton South*, 54–55; Peter Kolchin, *American Slavery*, 159; and Escott, *Slavery Remembered*, 81–85.

toward them, however, they recoiled at what they saw as a rebuke of their absolute authority. Alfred's voluntary return a few days later did nothing to change their minds. After two years of applauding his "appearance and manners," the family lost confidence in their courier. No longer did their correspondence report on Alfred's unsupervised travels around the state. Instead, it described his confinement to the Athens lot where his activities were monitored throughout the day. Likewise, the young Cobb's unwarranted act of violence shattered Alfred's illusions regarding his status with the family.

Given time, Alfred might have succeeded in restoring his previous position with the Cobb-Lamars, but unfortunately his decision to resist coincided with the family's departure for Washington. With his services no longer required in Athens, Mary Ann dispatched him back to the plantation. Alfred returned to an altered situation at home. After more than two years away, his brother, Floyd, had assumed his role as a wagon driver, and the plantation already held its needed allotment of hands.

John B. saw a place for Alfred on a new plantation he had ordered carved out of the swamps of Worth County. Alfred knew from reports of those already dispatched there that the wilderness near the Flint River had the potential to breed disease and become a death sentence. Although John B. gave no indication that he intended the assignment as punishment for Alfred's failure to conform to the family's expectations while working in Athens, Alfred found the very notion of his new assignment unbearable. Once again he ran away. This time he did not seek a cooling-off period as he had after being whipped for lending young Lamar's saddle. Rather, he determined to appeal directly to his owner for justice and mercy. Here too he pursued a mode of resistance often employed by the enslaved on Cobb-Lamar plantations. John B. recognized the tactic and had responded favorably in other instances. He rejected Alfred's appeal, however, because it posed a challenge to his authority rather than that of a hired overseer. In anticipation of Alfred's return to Athens, he instructed his nephew to have the runaway confined to jail and left there as punishment until he ordered his release. Damning Alfred's "case of big-head," he explained his determination to his nephew by saying that "his example will have a bad effect on the other negroes, until he is punished for his conduct."[17]

Alfred eventually made his way to the Cobb house in Athens but first

17. John B. Lamar to John A. Cobb II, November 17, 1857.

fled to Macon to plead his case to John B. After learning of John B.'s absence, he pushed on. He arrived in Athens to find young John A. Cobb resolved to obey his uncle's instructions but managed to escape and hide in "Mrs. Maxwell's stable." His reprieve proved brief. John A. discovered his hiding place, bound him, and transported him to jail. When reporting his success to his uncle, he noted that Alfred had abundant clothing and "four good Blankets," adding, "I think with that he can keep himself warm."[18]

Beating, binding, and incarceration failed to break Alfred's will to resist. Nor did the prospect of exile. John B. persisted in his decision to send the rebellious young man to the Worth Place, but Alfred remained watchful and within a matter of weeks fled the Worth County wilderness in a final bid for freedom.[19] His bid ended days later in the North Georgia mountains near Dahlonega. A local posse chased him for more than twelve hours, aided by A. B. Barker's pack of tracking dogs, kept "for the express Business of ketching Runaways." They captured him after a chase that extended more than fifty miles and ended near Cooper's Gap in the Blue Ridge Mountains. W. C. Cole, one of the pursuers, grudgingly acknowledged Alfred's courage, reporting, "he is a sounde fellow and can fite dogs with a vengeance."[20]

Confined in the Dahlonega jail, Alfred remained defiant. When his captors asked his name, he gave "Edward" as an alias. He even crafted a narrative that he had escaped another jail in an attempt to avoid punishment for murdering an enslaved man in Worth County. Ultimately his effort to confuse his captors failed when a man from Athens identified the

---

18. John A. Cobb II to John B. Lamar, November 30, [1857].

19. On running away, see John Hope Franklin and Loren Schweninger, *Runaway Slaves: Rebels on the Plantation* (New York: Oxford University Press, 1999). See also Barbara McCaskill, *Love, Liberation, and Escaping Slavery: William and Ellen Craft in Cultural Memory* (Athens: University of Georgia Press, 2015); Edward E. Baptist, *The Half Has Never Been Told: Slavery and the Making of American Capitalism* (New York: Basic Books, 2014), 168–69; Walter Johnson, *River of Dark Dreams: Slavery and Empire in the Cotton Kingdom* (Cambridge: Belknap Press of Harvard University Press, 2013), 225–34; Faust, *James Henry Hammond and the Old South*, 94–98; Escott, *Slavery Remembered*, 78, 81–85; John W. Blassingame, *The Slave Community: Plantation Life in the Antebellum South (New York: Oxford University Press, 1972)*, 196–206.

20. W. C. Cole to John B. Lamar, January 25, 1858. For accounts of runaways being hunted down and brutalized by hound dogs, see the recollections that former enslaved people James Green, Anderson Williams, Henry Waldon, Evie Herrin, Richard Johnson, Gabe Emmanuel, and others shared with Federal Writers' Project interviewers in the 1930s. James Mellon, ed., *Bullwhip Days: The Slaves Remember* (New York: Weidenfeld & Nicholson, 1988), 298–302. See also Johnson, *River of Dark Dreams*, 234–40; Franklin and Schweninger, *Runaway Slaves*, 160–64.

prisoner and knocked most of his story to pieces. Frustrated at every turn, Alfred still refused to make life easy for his jailers. W. C. Cole complained to John B., "The fact is the Boy is a smart Rascal and must Be Jailed every Nite and Handcufft during the day and a eye on him all the time."[21]

His captors soon returned Alfred to John B. in Macon. The family pondered selling him in the New Orleans slave market but decided to return him to Sumter County instead.[22] Their restraint in dealing with Alfred might have reflected a sense that at some level his grievance had merit. Alfred never doubted that it did. Indeed, Mary Ann recognized that her son had acted improperly, especially given that she had previously admonished him for striking a different enslaved person. Still, because Alfred had directly challenged the authority of John B., rather than that of an overseer such as Stancil Barwick, the family would not permit him to fully gain what he sought. Reassignment to Sumter denied him what he most wanted but spared him what he most feared. Although he did not get his wish of returning to live in Athens, his resolute determination to resist abusive treatment allowed him to secure a return to his original home rather than banishment in the swamps of Worth County.

The ability of John B., Howell, and Mary Ann to settle on a compromise for Alfred was made possible by their extraordinary wealth and power. Less affluent masters might have resorted to extreme violence or forced sales to try to make a success of owning the few people they did, but the Cobb-Lamars could afford to try to live up to their oft-stated goal of being more humane.[23] They could afford to wrestle with these issues, seek out middle ground, and settle on compromises that they thought seemed fair. Their attempts, however, often left them befuddled by what they saw as an endless stream of insubordination. In private moments, Mary Ann vented to her husband about her inability to understand the gap between her good intentions and the chaos with which she was repaid. Her orderly household sometimes felt like a teetering house of cards in which every small and individual resistance could only be understood in concert with countless others. "Alfred *ran* away soon after you left and Lucius has been making accts at the cake & candy shop," she wrote to Howell, noting also, "Rachel does not want to go to the plantation. Sylvia was un-

21. W. C. Cole to John B. Lamar, January 25, 1858.
22. For the New Orleans slave market, see Walter Johnson, *Soul by Soul: Life inside the Antebellum Slave Market* (Cambridge: Harvard University Press, 2003).
23. John B. Lamar to Howell Cobb, August 16, 1837; Howell Cobb to Mary Ann Cobb, December 13, 1850; Mary Ann Cobb to John A. Cobb II, August 20, 1858.

happy for awhile but seems *resigned* to her fate, her girls likewise. . . . Everything is deranged about the house . . . and everything and everybody is *mixed up* so that there is no head or foot, no mistress or maid."[24]

As seen in the cases of Sylvia, Rachel, George, Alfred, and even Lucius, those enslaved by the family understood that their owners' status and inclination allowed broad spaces for resistance before the consequences became dire. While the Cobb-Lamars tolerated a certain degree of resistance from those they enslaved, they viewed themselves as the ultimate arbiters and brooked no opposition to their final decrees. Household laborers who crossed this line, such as Alfred or Rachel, faced banishment to far-off plantations. For some, this would have been a terrible outcome. For others, however, the return to the plantation meant reunion with family and friends. A teenage cook named Berry Robinson, for instance, consciously pursued an agenda aimed at eliciting exactly this "punishment."

Berry was the son of Nancy Florida and Jerry Robinson. He was born prior to the Cobb-Lamars moving him, his siblings, his parents, and some three dozen other enslaved people from Florida to the Spring Creek Plantation in Sumter County in the mid-1840s.[25] Because Nancy was a cook, John B. ultimately brought Berry to Macon to begin working in the kitchen of the Bear's Den. In 1854 he sent Berry to the home of his cousin Sarah Lamar Rees of Americus, to continue Berry's training.[26] For several weeks a series of positive reports on his aptitude, attitude, and conduct flowed from Sarah's pen. After only eight days, she confidently declared to John B., "You were never in my opinion more correct in your judgement than in selecting Berry as one to make a cook of . . . he is doing his best and I think will continue to do so." She felt compelled to add,

---

24. Mary Ann Cobb to Howell Cobb, July 10, 1857.

25. The enslaved community that the Cobb-Lamars moved to Sumter County represented their share of the estate of their maternal uncle, William Robinson, who died in 1844. Noting that the distribution of enslaved labor on their existing plantations already yielded maximum profitability, John B. purchased the first of the family's seven plantations in Southwest Georgia. Doing so enabled the Cobb-Lamars to expand the geographic scope of their agricultural enterprise, prevent the separation of this enslaved community, and create a space where their labor would be profitable. John B. Lamar to Howell Cobb, December 10, 1844, December 23, 1844, and February 17, 1845; John B. Lamar to Mary Ann Cobb, December 12, 1844, March 3, 1845, and January 23, 1846; Andrew Jackson Lamar to John B. Lamar, December 12, 1845.

26. Sarah Ann Lamar Rees (November 26, 1807–September 25, 1872), a cousin of Mary Ann Cobb and John B. Lamar, lived in Americus with her husband Albert Rees (ca. 1802–October 2, 1876), a physician.

"I do not covet your property or anyone else's. I do wish however that I had just such a boy as Berry."[27]

After six months of exemplary service in Sarah's kitchen, Berry sought permission to visit his family back at Spring Creek. Sarah denied his request and instructed him that he would need to delay the trip until fall. Despite fewer than twenty miles separating the Rees home and the plantation, she gave the excuse that she feared for his health in traveling during the summer malarial season. While she believed she acted out of concern for his safety, he understood her denial as a transgression of one of the agreements the Cobb-Lamars had with the people they enslaved. Sarah noted a marked change in his behavior, writing to her cousin, "He has not cooked as well of late and himself and kitchen I have had to complain of not being as neat as formerly."[28] From this point on, Berry's relations with the Rees family deteriorated as his acts of resistance gradually expanded from poor cooking and slovenliness to outright refusal to obey instructions—unless compelled by anger—and refusal to speak to their children.

As Berry's resistance persisted, Rees escalated her efforts to regulate his behavior. She ordered him not to leave the lot at night without permission but promised to give him a pass two or three times per week if he did his work properly. Instead Berry rarely spent a night in his quarters. To his nighttime companions, he mocked her efforts to control him. He refused to keep himself clean and only performed his assignments when she grew angry with him. He gambled away or in some instances simply destroyed the allotment of clothing she gave him. Eventually he pushed the situation to a crisis when a neighbor caught him "cutting off a favorite dogs foot."[29] Rees and her husband paid the neighbor fifty dollars to compensate for the mutilation of the beloved animal. Frustrated, her husband "gave him a little switching," but it altered Berry's behavior not one whit.[30] They then agreed to John B.'s suggestion to return Berry to Spring Creek, where the overseer could break him of his propensity for disobedience.

Berry had manipulated Rees and John B. into providing him that which he most desired: a return to his family. Once back at Spring Creek, the overseer found no need to discipline him. When, after a few weeks,

27. Sarah Rees to John B. Lamar, May 30, 1854.
28. Sarah Rees to John B. Lamar, July 21, 1854.
29. Sarah Rees to John B. Lamar, November 3, 1854.
30. Sarah Rees to John B. Lamar, December 18, 1854.

the overseer returned him to the Rees home, Berry resumed his resistance. Once more confronted about his behavior, he burst into tears and declared that he "did not want to come from home" and preferred life on the plantation.[31] He followed this declaration with a refusal to obey any orders or do any work for several days despite more switching by her husband. Rees accused the overseer of urging him to continue his resistance in order to gain an additional worker. Finally she sought John B.'s permission to have the town marshal whip him. It is not clear whether he gave his consent, but Rees threatened Berry that if forced to this extreme she would insure that "he should be in a good humor before he was let off and willing to do anything I ordered."[32]

Confronted with the very real threat of being lashed by the marshal rather than ineffectually switched by Dr. Rees, Berry wisely shifted his tactics from outright rebellion to low-intensity resistance. Rees reported that he now went about his assigned tasks "whistling and singing" but still failed to keep himself or the kitchen clean and continued to break an alarming number of dishes.[33] Within two months, however, he resumed a stance of open defiance. Rees complained that he had resumed his habits of staying up all night and gambling. When she confined him in the dairy, he broke out. She wrote her cousin and pleaded for him to come to Americus to handle the situation. When John B. failed to respond, she finally called upon the marshal in late October. Following the whipping, Berry ran away.

In all likelihood, Berry returned to the vicinity of Spring Creek. Sarah Rees complained to John B., "[We both know that] he will be taken care of by The Negroes at some of your places," but she urged him to employ harsher measures than the Cobb-Lamars normally employed.[34] She would not be mocked: "I think if The Overseer will punish him well and bring him back tied this may mortify him and convince him he cannot have his own way altogether and that he has not set either yourself or myself at defiance."[35] Yet John B. declined to give her the satisfaction she demanded. Defeated, she permanently returned Berry to her cousin.

31. Sarah Rees to John B. Lamar, March 6, 1855.

32. Sarah Rees to John B. Lamar, March 22, 1855.

33. Sarah Rees to John B. Lamar, March 22, 1855.

34. Sarah Rees to John B. Lamar, November 8, 1855. For enslaved communities aiding individuals who had left the plantation without permission, see Daina Ramey Berry, *The Price for Their Pound of Flesh* (Boston: Beacon Press, 2017), 17, 61–62; Kaye, *Joining Places*, 129–32; Franklin and Schweninger, *Runaway Slaves*, 100, 102.

35. Sarah Rees to John B. Lamar, November 8, 1855.

For his part, having secured his objective of returning home, Berry ceased his resistance. Although the Rees household contained other enslaved people, Berry apparently did not establish close relationships with them. His sense of isolation left him displaced and alone. Indeed, much of his sneaking out to associate with other enslaved people in Americus might have reflected his drive to form friendships and reestablish a sense of belonging.[36] Yet, as other instances have demonstrated, remaining connected through the network and being there were different things. Those who were separated could keep up with news of family and friends or even remain in contact, but that small mercy was indivisible from the knowledge that their everyday lives went on despite the absences.

For a teenage boy like Berry, this developing awareness had to have been excruciatingly painful. His sobbing pleas to be returned to his family were reported by Sarah as an example of the trouble she was having managing him, but they may also reveal much about what he understood about the true cost of bondage. The wounds of separation often proved even more severe and permanent than wounds of the lash. In the midst of his struggle to be returned home to his family, Berry had learned through the informal Cobb-Lamar network that his mother, Nancy, had died at Spring Creek in August 1855. After a lifetime by her side, this period of exile at the end of childhood left him absent from her deathbed. He could never reclaim the time with her he had lost or have an opportunity to say goodbye or to see her again.

Forced separation from family also contributed to the most shocking case of violence committed by someone the Cobb-Lamars enslaved. Sylvia's teenage daughter Polly was one of the two girls at the heart of Sylvia's fracture with Mary Ann in 1848. Polly and her sister Eliza had been sent to stay with their grandmother at Cherry Hill rather than joining their mother and brothers at the Cowpens in 1844. Sylvia's service over the next four years revolved around an effort to renegotiate her family's

---

36. For the ways in which the enslaved used urban spaces to create and maintain connections that extended beyond a single household or establishment, see Maurie D. McInnis, "Life in the Yard," chap. 8 in *The Politics of Taste in Antebellum Charleston* (Chapel Hill: University of North Carolina Press, 2005); John Michael Vlatch, "'Without Recourse to Owners': The Architecture of Urban Slavery in the Antebellum South," *Perspectives in Vernacular Architecture* 6 (1997): 157–59; Whittington B. Johnson, *Black Savannah, 1788–1864* (Fayetteville: University of Arkansas Press, 1996), 119–21; Bernard E. Powers, Jr., "Slavery in Antebellum Charleston," chap. 1 in *Black Charlestonians: A Social History, 1822–1885* (Fayetteville: University of Arkansas Press, 1994); and Richard C. Wade, *Slavery in the Cities: The South, 1820–1860* (New York: Oxford University Press, 1964), 143–55.

situation in light of her sense that Mary Ann had been harsh in separating her from her children. Her attempts to have first Eliza and then Polly returned to Athens in 1848 initially proved successful. Immediately after Polly's arrival in January 1849, Mary Ann began to hire her as a day laborer to neighbors.[37] This arrangement allowed her to return to her mother and sister each night.

Within a matter of days, however, Mary Ann discovered Sylvia's maneuvers to bring her mother to join the rest of the family in Athens. By midwinter, Polly had been removed from the household and leased out to live with the Lampkin family across town in the Franklin House Hotel. She found this arrangement much less agreeable. She was now not only separated from her grandmother at Cherry Hill but also removed from the comfort of being with her mother and sister. She viewed this relocation as a violation of Mary Ann's pledge to reunite the family.

Polly was leased to Terrell and America Lampkin to care for their infant daughter, Willianna. From the beginning, however, she constantly acted in ways intended to challenge her employers. Polly escalated expressions of her displeasure with the situation by loudly talking with any and every enslaved person she could find, slapping another enslaved girl, speaking crossly to white children, and repeatedly dumping her full chamber pot out of an upper window so the contents blew back into the lower dining room or onto the piano in the drawing room. This resistance continued even in public. "I never carried Polly anywhere with me, that I did not see, that her conduct whilst there, was displeasing," America complained to Mary Ann. The young mother insisted that she thought the difficulty "proceeded more from thickness of skull, than from depravity of heart," but she also admitted that she had failed to confront Polly from fear, writing, "If I were strict with her, it would make her unkind to my child when out of my sight, of which I have always had a great horror."[38]

When the Lampkins relocated that summer to Mrs. Wooldridge's

---

37. On hiring out, see John J. Zamborney, *Slaves for Hire: Renting Enslaved Laborers in Antebellum Virginia* (Baton Rouge: Louisiana State University Press, 2012); Jonathan D. Martin, *Divided Mastery: Slave Hiring in the American South* (Cambridge: Harvard University Press, 2004). See also Stephanie E. Jones-Rogers, *They Were Her Property: White Women as Slave Owners in the American South* (New Haven: Yale University Press, 2019), 66–68; Berry, *Swing the Sickle for the Harvest Is Ripe*, 114–15, 119; William A. Byrne, "The Hiring of Woodson, Slave Carpenter of Savannah," *Georgia Historical Quarterly* 77, no. 2 (Summer 1993): 249–50; Ira Berlin, *Slaves without Masters: The Free Negro in the Antebellum South* (New York: New Press, 1974), 228–39, 350–51; Wade, *Slavery in the Cities*, 38–54.

38. America Lampkin to Mary Ann Cobb, June 23, 1849.

nearby boardinghouse, Polly's actions grew more extreme and increasingly violent. America finally admonished her for unacceptable behavior. Just as the young mother had feared, Willianna now became the primary target of Polly's frustrations. One night, when the baby was "fretful from teething," Polly removed her from her crib after the rest of the house had retired for the evening. Within moments, the dozing parents awakened to the sound of "the hardest fall I ever knew a baby to have, followed by terrible screams." The infant screamed for ninety minutes before being overtaken by vomiting, "which lasted until through exhaustion she went to sleep but passed a bad night." Believing Polly guilty of gross negligence, if not something worse, America nonetheless refrained from castigating the teenage girl because she "looked very sorry."[39] When Terrell declared his intention of returning Polly to Mary Ann, America protested and prevented it.

America's intervention on Polly's behalf proved a tragic mistake. Two or three evenings later, while the Lampkins and the other boarders relaxed in the parlor following tea, "we heard another fall and scream." The entire household rushed upstairs to find Polly "shaking the baby."[40] Polly denied that she had dropped the infant and insisted that the noise had been caused by a dropped milk bottle. No one present believed her story.

Willianna's injuries appeared far more severe following this second incident. America wrote to Mary Ann, "The baby only gave one scream, and fell asleep from [which] I tried to raise her not liking the symptoms, but we could not succeed by playing and talking to her in awaking her. The next morning she looked heavy and bad, and she has not been well since." Finally, after weeks of leaving their helpless infant to abuse, Terrell Lampkin whipped Polly and sent her back to the Cobbs. In America's long explanation to Mary Ann of their causes for sending her home, she related that she had confronted Polly to explain the decision to dismiss her. Even then Polly remained defiant. America told her, "I would be a strange mother not to find some fault with a servant who had three times thrown my baby down, that I knew of, and how many times beside I am not aware of," but Polly, America told Mary Ann, "wished to have all the conversation to herself and I to listen." Driven to anger by Polly's persistence, America ordered her to be silent. "Finding that she would not," she wrote, "I was under the necessity of several times slapping her." In

---

39. Ibid.
40. Ibid.

surveying the wreckage of Polly's service, the young mother could only voice the hope that "if [Willianna] ever gets over the falls she receives I shall be thankful indeed."[41] This hope proved as ill-placed as her faith in Polly's affection for her child. Willianna Lampkin died six weeks later of "Spinal Aff[liction]."[42]

Mary Ann believed that the fault for Polly's offence rested on lax supervision. She initially drafted a vehement response to America's litany of misbehavior, blaming the young mother of gross mismanagement. After further consideration, however, she tendered a coldly formal note. "I am obliged to you for returning her to me," she wrote, and directed the Lampkins how to settle their account.[43] They did as instructed. Polly suffered no further consequences. She was returned to the Cobb household, where she remained with her mother and sister for six months before Mary Ann began to hire her out again.

Just as when those enslaved at the Hurricane attempted to poison Simon Ruff, Mary Ann found Polly's actions unacceptable but not an affront to her rule. She appeared to view the Lampkins as she would a plantation overseer. Polly recognized and exploited this incongruity. Like others who had been hired out, she and Berry defied their intermediate supervisors and found that their masters passively acquiesced. Berry had been forced by Sarah Rees to listen as she read aloud her letters of complaint to John B. but likely felt encouraged each time his owner declined to intervene beyond suggesting that she return him to Spring Creek.[44] Yet Alfred learned, as had Sylvia and Rachel, that direct challenges to his owners enjoyed no such tolerance. No other person enslaved by the Cobb-Lamars so flagrantly refused to accept the family's authority to decide the course of his life. Alfred's decision to run, rather than accept banishment to Worth County, was a revolutionary act. Others who resisted sought to make the conditions of their bondage more tolerable; Alfred's bid for freedom was an utter repudiation of the entire unjust system.

The Cobb-Lamars wanted to believe they had absolute power over their chattels. Acts of resistance by those they held in bondage, however,

41. Ibid.

42. U.S. Census, 1850, Clarke County, Georgia, mortality schedule, August 11, 1849, Willianna Lampkin.

43. Mary Ann Cobb to America Lampkin, June 26, 1849.

44. For Rees forcing Berry to listen to her letters of complaint, see Sarah Rees to John B. Lamar, June 9, 1855.

demonstrated that their control teetered on the willingness of the enslaved to comply.

══════════════

Mary Ann Cobb to Howell Cobb

Athens, February 1, 1837

A letter came to you yesterday ... from the overseer[45]. ... He suspects some of the negroes of an attempt to *trick him* (as he calls it) and had discovered from whom they obtained the *stuff*, it being a negro doctor belonging to Mr. Tufts of Jones county. I am afraid you will have some trouble before you can bring the negroes under subordination, after having been so long without a *real master* (your title until late being only nominal) I suspect you will have to resort to some severe manner of treatment before you can compel them to know their places. They are fully in the belief that they can do as they please as everyone says that they have such a kind master.

Simon Ruff to Howell Cobb

Hurricane Plantation, April 5, 1837

I have Received your letter of 28 March and am as much astonished at your letter as you was at mine. It contained things that I did not Expect, you say you know that the Negroes can be managed without cruelty. You are not aware off the disposition off three or four off the negroes on the place. It has allways been their character to trouble the overseer. They are what I call murderers. They have nearly killed two men before I came on the place, for my own part I could manage them if I had my way. You say you will not suffer any thing like cruelty. You know that Negroes will obey masters when numbers will not an overseer. If I let them go there way you will say that I am of no acount. I am bound to treat them in a humane manner which I have tried to do as much as I could. I think you will find some here that you could not treat in a humane manner yourself if

───────────

45. Simon Ruff.

you was on the place. You say in annother part of your letter if I cannot Get on with them without making threats to take lives we had best part at once. I think it to be the best plan if I stay here. I will not suffer the Negroes to trample on me.[46]

John B. Lamar to Howell Cobb
Macon, August 16, 1837

Your boy Ellick ran away from your overseer & came to me some days ago. I ordered him to go back, but he was very unwilling to do so. And said from the general conduct of the overseer to him he was sure of being unmercifully beaten if he returned. I was convinced that if I sent him back, that he would run away & lie out, & I disliked to put him in jail on many accounts, so I ordered him to go to my place & stay until I should be advised by you what to do with him. I will pay you his hire in the meanwhile or keep him during the balance of the year as you like. . . .

Louis a boy of yours ranaway about 3 months ago & came over here. I wrote a letter recommending him to the clemency of the overseer & sent him home. The overseer however whipped him severely. This circumstance has frightened Ellick together with a belief that the overseer is predisposed to use him worse than the rest. I am disposed to believe that your overseer is not the proper person for your place. . . . And the circumstance of his not being able to manage his negroes [without] running them off is evidence of his incapacity with me.

John B. Lamar to Mary Ann Cobb
Macon, October 21, 1846

At the Hurricane, I have a mulish, obstinate creature who does everything in an indirect way to thwart me. On account of his severity I shall discharge him on the 1st of January & his knowledge of this fact, leaving him nothing to hope for, he now tries every round about way to disappoint me. . . . He is sufficiently ingenious to find an excuse for all this, which renders it the more provoking. As no man has ever been known to

---

46. Ruff was fired later that year. David Gibson replaced him as overseer that November. See contract between Howell Cobb and David Gibson, November 24, 1837.

come out of a contest with an overseer without loss, I feel no disposition to run against the experience of everybody as long as evils are sufferable, & I must bear yet a little longer. Particularly as he obeys sufficiently to treat the negroes humanely of late. But take him all in all he has tried my temper a little farther than I would suffer it to be stretched by anybody except the *aristocracy* of middle Georgia—*Overseers.*

John B. Lamar to Mary Ann Cobb
Macon, December 28, 1848

Yours of the 26th came to hand yesterday. In compliance with your request I have sent over after little Polly, so as to have her here to go up with Jim Stewart when he comes after the carriage. Such articles as she is obliged to have she will take along with her & when the waggon comes to Macon, the balance can be bought here & sent by the railroad. I think Aunt Sylvia in her great desire to get her daughter, manifests a selfish disregard for an aged parent she has at the plantation. When Polly leaves, the old woman will have no relation with her.

Mary Ann Cobb to Howell Cobb
Athens, January 10, 1849

Polly came in the carriage with James on Saturday. She is strong, hearty and well grown. I have sent her out for two days now to get work until I can get a place for her for the year. . . . Sylvia is as happy as she can be, 10 years seem to have been added to her life, judging from her willingness to work, and an increased nimbleness. It is well to gratify servants sometimes, and better still to make good your promises to them, as it holds out to them in future a certain reward.

America Lampkin[47] to Mary Ann Cobb

Athens, June 23, [1849][48]

Dear Cousin Marianne,

I am under the necessity of sending Polly home, and do not wish to do so, without making you acquainted with various occurrences, which have recently taken place.

When Polly first came to me, I was astonished to find her decidedly the reverse of what I had expected, being very indolent besides being very much inclined to impertinence in her actions to grown persons, and in her speech to small children, speaking to them as she would to any little negro, when I perceived this I struck out a course of action for myself which until about two weeks since I have implicitly followed, notwithstanding the many remonstrances I received from relations and others, who felt themselves privileged to take a liberty of that sort, it was this never to notice anything that she did, pass it by, as though I did not perceive it, fearing that if I were strict with her, it would make her unkind to my child when out of my sight, of which I have always had a great horror. I also thought that the many errors of which she was guilty, proceeded from a great lack of sense, and often when I would be tempted to reprove her I would be deterred therefrom thinking it proceeded more from thickness of skull, than from depravity of heart. I never carried Polly anywhere with me, that I did not see, that her conduct whilst there, was displeasing, she would stand in passages, hail every negro she saw, and have a loud chat with them, not ten steps from the family, or say something cross to the white children, which made me feel awkward fearing that if I scolded her, she in turn would be cross to the baby. I would therefore apologize and perhaps say that her great love for, and care of the baby was my chief reason for permitting her to act so. Finding our room at the Franklin House[49] getting too warm and not succeeding in getting another that we liked we concluded to remove to Mrs. Wooldridges[50] where

---

47. America Flournoy Lampkin (ca. 1825–August 3, 1903) was a distant relative of Howell Cobb.

48. America mistakenly misdated this letter as 1848; the context of the following series of letters make clear that this incident took place in June 1849.

49. Built around 1845, the Franklin House (see map 2) served as a hotel, with mercantile shops on the first floor.

50. Maria Wooldridge operated a boarding house and school (see map 2), which the older Cobb boys attended. *Southern Whig* (Athens), January 24, 1850; Augustus Longstreet

we could get a delightful room, Polly was violently opposed to coming for what reason I could not imagine although I believe now that she liked the publicity of the Franklin House.

A night or two after our removal Polly as has been her custom found the baby has been fretful from teething, took her out of her crib (it was only a minute or so after we had gone to bed). I do not know why it was that I got into a doze, from which I was awakened by the hardest fall I ever knew a baby have, followed by terrible screams. We both jumped out of bed, and I seized the baby who screamed at intervals for an hour and a half at the end of which time she was taken with vomiting which lasted until through exhaustion she went to sleep but passed a bad night. I never even told Polly that she was careless in letting the baby fall out of her lap, for she looked very sorry and I thought *was*. Mr. Lampkin[51] told her she should go home in the morning but I interceded for her and he allowed her to stay. Some two or three evenings after that, just after tea and while we were in the parlor we heard another fall and scream, at which everyone in the room was startled, on running upstairs Polly was shaking the baby, she denied that the baby had fallen and said that it was the bottle of milk. The baby only gave one scream, and fell asleep from [which] I tried to raise her not liking the symptoms, but we could not succeed by playing and talking to her in awaking her. The next morning she looked heavy and bad, and has not been well since ([Polly] told a lady downtown that she did let her fall, but was afraid to say so, as Terrell had promised to punish her the next time such a thing happened, and send her home after that). No one but a *Mother* can know what anxiety of mind I suffered if she was out of my sight one minute, and there was the least noise I was startled thinking it was the baby. I was therefore under the necessity of making her stay just by me if I went upstairs, made her go with me if downstairs likewise. Thursday morning I wished to step out of doors but waited until someone came in the room fearing to leave Polly alone with the baby. She finally went to sleep. I left the home scarcely had I done so when I had to run back, as quick as I could attracted by the screams of the baby, and found Mrs. Wooldridge had left the school room, and the family had assembled from different

---

Hull, *Annals of Athens, 1801–1901* (Athens: Banner Job Office, 1906), 200.

51. Terrell Lampkin (October 1823–December 3, 1867) was a part owner of the *Southern Whig* newspaper and Job Printing Office located on Broad Street in Athens. *Southern Whig,* May 31, 1849; *Southern Whig,* July 11, 1850. See also Charlotte Thomas Marshall, *Oconee Hill Cemetery of Athens, Georgia,* vol. 1 (Athens, Ga.: Athens Historical Society, 2009), 219; Earnest C. Hynds, *Antebellum Athens and Clarke County, Georgia* (Athens: University of Georgia Press, 1974), 58.

parts of the house on account of the noise, and screams. Polly said that the sponge had choked the baby, I asked her if that had caused her to scream, so she knew she was telling an untruth. I did not tell Terrell of it. He found it out however, and she assigned to him as a reason of the noise, that she stumbled once and threw down a chair, the only chair near the bed was an immense rocking chair, which she could not easily overturn, unless she had taken both hands to it, which she could not do unless she had laid the baby down. I think myself she fell over the chair and hurt the baby very much for she was fretful and unwell all day. Indeed if she ever gets over the falls she receives I shall be thankful indeed. The same night she let her fall she carried her upstairs to get her milk. The first story was dark with the exception of the parlor from which a light provided which made the staircase very discernable. Everyone was in the basement, with the exception of one of the family who having eat little supper was sitting in a room looking on the staircase as she went upstairs. He saw her distinctly slap Willianna's face and from things which I have since heard she has I've no doubt always treated her badly, and completely deceived me who thought that if ever child was loved by its nurse that child was by hers. I think the reason she acted so badly since I have been here is that I have several times reproved her for the course she was pursuing. The day after we came her[e] I felt myself called upon to speak to her of the manner in which she would stand laughing, and talking aloud to the servants and in a loud tone of voice taking it upon herself to rule the small servants, and even went so far as to slap Mrs. Wooldridge little girl, I told her that she ought to remember that we were in a private house and none of the servants but herself acted as she did, and it would not do, she complained very much of [a] little servant about seven. I told her if she acted wrong to go and tell her mistress, not to threatening to slap her and go quarreling all about the house. I found that she threw her slop water through the room window into the yard half of which generally fell in the dining room and if the drawing room window was open a part of it spattered the carpet and piano. I saw her one morning throw it within a foot of Mrs. Wooldridges scholars and spoke to her about it twice before she stopped it.

Last Saturday night just before I went to bed, I told her to attend to the chamber, she deliberately threw it out of the window and put it away without washing it. She found out that Mrs W was neat about her home and she took especial pleasure in making as much dirt as she could throwing milk about the house squeezing the sponge filled with milk over the clean passage and last night turned the pitcher upside down so that the milk might drain all over the newly scoured back piazza. At half past nine I wanted to go up stairs and sent for Polly who said she had not boiled the milk. I told her she had had time to boil it. She very cooly informed me that I knew nothing about what time she had had to boil it. I felt myself getting vexed but as I thought that was a good time to talk to her as we intended sending her home I gave her to understand that the reason of my recent strictness was not owing to any interference of Mrs W as she said, but to my own ideas of right, and wrong, and that had I not known that she was both unkind, and careless, with Willianna I should have treated her with the indulgence I used to, but now the case was otherwise and I would be a strange mother not to find some fault with a servant who had three times thrown my baby down, that I knew of, and how many times beside I am not aware of. She wished to have all the conversation to herself and I to listen, but as I did not exactly coincide with her, I told her to stop and let me finish. Finding that she would not I was under the necessity of several times slapping her. When Mr. Lampkin came home he told her that she must today leave which I was glad to hear, as I would rather be my own nurse than have such a girl about. I write at length because I do not know when I shall see you the walk being long.

After I had finished this and while Terrell was reading it she in a rage shook the baby against his chair, he could not stand this and although he had not for all her ill treatment to the baby intended punishing her unless she had done something to call for it yet he gave her a few stripes. Mr Lampkin wishes me to say that if he exacts it he will pay the whole years rent and settle with John[52] at any time.

—America F. Lampkin

You will find this scarcely readable my excuse is that the baby has the thrush and frets a great deal and as she is in the room with me makes writing quite a task.

---

52. John B. Cobb (February 3, 1826–November 21, 1893) was Howell Cobb's youngest brother. An entrepreneur and landlord, he sometimes acted as Howell's and Mary Ann's business agent. He later enlisted in his brother T. R. R. Cobb's Georgia Legion and rose to the rank of major during the Civil War. Marshall, *Oconee Hill Cemetery of Athens*, 232; Hull, *Annals of Athens, 1801–1901*, 254.

Mary Ann Cobb to America Lampkin [not sent]

Athens, [June 1849]

I have intentionally delayed answering your letter for a day, because I would not allow myself to give expression to the feelings of just indignation and surprize which were excited in me by the perusal of its contents.

If you are dissatissfied with Polly I am exceedingly obliged to you for returning her to me—for I have an utter horror of having my servants employed by those who are not favorably disposed to them—for in all cases when prejudice and dislike exist the most trivial actions of a servant will be construed with the worst intentions. . . .

No one can read your letter without discerning plainly that all these disturbances have arisen since your removal from the Franklin House, and the cause is equally perceptible—and as long as you allow the officious intermeddling of friends in your private matters, you will have the same complaint to urge against the best servants you may hire, for no angels purity would scarcely withstand the corrupting influence . . . which is most generally practiced in a private boarding house. . . .

Hoping that your fears about your infant having been unnecessarily excited, and that you may be successful in finding a nurse to suit you as well [as] Polly did untill at the Franklin House.

Mary Ann Cobb to America Lampkin

Athens, June 26, 1849

Your letter of the 24th inst. was handed me by Polly. I am obliged to you for returning her to me, since she has ceased to give you satisfaction.

Mr. Lampkin will please call upon Mr. Jno B. Cobb and settle with him for the time that Polly *has served* you.

1850 U.S. Census Mortality Schedule for Athens, Georgia*

NAME OF EVERY PERSON WHO DIED during the Year ending 1st June, 1850, whose usual Place of Abode at the Time of his Death was in this Family	Description				PLACE OF BIRTH Naming the State, Territory, or Country	The Month in which this Person died	DISEASE, OR CAUSE OF DEATH	Number of DAYS ILL
	Age	Sex	Color (White, black, or mulatto)	Free or Slave				
Willianna Lampkin	9/12	F	W		Georgia	Aug	Spinal Aff	2m

*The mortality schedule was part of the U.S. Census taken each decade, but it recorded only the deaths of residents who died the previous year. Willianna's death in August 1849, two months after the incident recorded in her mother's letter, is recorded as part of the 1850 census.

John B. Lamar to Mary Ann Cobb

Macon, November 30, 1851

During my absence at Milledgeville some villain poisoned two of my best Dogs—viz Barnam & Boy.[53] They have gone to that bourne whence no dog ever returns & left numerous friends to bewail their untimely end. Some thief who found them too vigilant for him to rob my smoke house, found it necessary to carry on his trade, to put them out of the way. I had but one Turkey, one lone Gobler awaiting thanksgiving day, & the night the Dogs died, he took his departure, to grace some other table.

Mary Ann Cobb to John B. Lamar

Moreton Hampstead,[54] March 14, 1853

On Mr Eli Whidden's return from Macon with his negro woman, he brought rather doleful news from [the] plantations . . . in Sumter Co:

> Some 10 or 15 negro men runaway, and a part of them having been arrested were in the Macon jail, and still worse 40 bags of false picked cotton returned to you from Liverpool.

I sincerely hope there is considerable exaggeration in these statements. The latter clause came so heavily upon me that I lost *one* dinner by it. I know it will not lessen the weight of the trouble which is incident to such disclosures, but it affords . . . a palpable demonstration of my heart's sympathy. . . . I cannot but hope that there is much falsity in the news.

---

53. In 1850 John B. Lamar took his nephews John A. and Lamar Cobb to New York and Philadelphia, where they saw P. T. Barnum's traveling exhibition. John B. Lamar to Mary Ann Cobb, April 25, 1850 (see chapter 1).

54. The Washington County plantation of Oliver and Sarah Prince, cousins of the Cobb family. Sarah Prince's letter on the death of Bob Scott is cited in chapter 2.

John B. Lamar to Mary Ann Cobb
Macon, January 5, 1854

I was sorry to hear that poor old Bob had died. He carries the sincere regret of many a friend to his long home. What have you thought about a carriage driver? If you have no other arrangement, there is a boy named Alfred in Sumter, about 19 yrs old or thereabouts, a . . . lively, but steady chap, of the old Lev stock, being a grandson on the mothers side of that worthy individual and a son of Abram you (or anybody else) own & a brother of Floyd the boy I spoke of sending you once. You may think him over young for a carriage driver, but he is a *regular waggoner* & drives with the cotton to Montezuma & drove his waggon up here at Christmas with the negro's Nankin crop & back. So you see he has experience. I had him here for several months about six years ago, at the time he got his arm broke, following Ben Brewers waggon, as waggon boy, to have the Dr attend to him & thought him a reliable sort of chap. If you would like to take him, I can put Floyd in his place & make a waggoner of him, as I think any of that "breed" will answer in any place they are put. Alfred is the only boy I know of that I could recommend.

John B. Lamar to Mary Ann Cobb
Macon, April 6, 1854

I have given notice to your carriage driver that is to be—viz Alfred, that I shall take him away, when I go down in May to give out summer clothes. I would have sent him to you sooner, but Willis' bone-felon on his thumb has been very hard to cure & he is here under treatment yet & will be for 3 or 4 weeks & I could not take another able hand out of the crop until he goes back.

From the character Alfred bears I expect he will suit you. He is intelligent & obedient, & faithful. If there is any thing in breeds of people, he ought to make a good servant as he comes of good stock in both sides of the house. I think I had rather have Abram & Hetty (his father & mother) & their children, than any family of negroes of the same number I ever saw. Alfred is about 19 years old.

Sarah A. Rees to John B. Lamar

Americus, May 11, 1854

I wish you now to send Berry[55] to me and I will put him at once in the kitchen. . . . I shall need to have Berry as we have let Sampson go and Judy has an infant two days old.

Sarah A. Rees to John B. Lamar

Americus, May 22, 1854

Berry came yesterday in good spirits. . . . I find him up and ready to do this morning. I told him I wished in a short time to have him as good a cook as I am myself, and that I was inclined to think him smart enough to learn anything. He says he will do his best, and I assure you if I have health it shall not be my fault if he does not cook well. I will give him a list of such as he has learned when he leaves and you can send him down of a summer to learn to do other things if he leaves before learning all I can teach him. He ought to be here in season for making souse & sausages and calfs feet or hogs feet jellies, to prepare mince meats to make Buckwheat cakes, prepare large hominy [and] make hashes and many winter dishes.

Sarah A. Rees to John B. Lamar

Americus, May 30, 1854

I now write to tell you of Berry. You were never in my opinion more correct in your judgement than in selecting Berry as one to make a cook of. I have kept him cooking three meals a day since Wednesday last, and I have done no sewing have been attending to the cooking, and yesterday I was all day in the kitchen making several varieties of cakes and I have not been as much complimented in a long while as by Berry. He says he does not see any reason why anyone cannot learn to cook who will be in the

---

55. Berry's family lived on a Sumter County plantation, but he had lived at the Bear's Den since at least 1851 and had been a playmate of the Cobb boys during their extended visits to their uncle's home. John B. Lamar to Mary Ann Cobb, March 20, 1851.

kitchen with me. . . . he says Uncle Davy[56] told him he would go home for him to learn him to cook, but he says, Miss Sarah I dont think it will take me long to beat Uncle Davy, & he wont like it neither said Berry, he says Uncle Davy has been four years at it and Mars John hardly ever eats his biscuits and he never makes any good cake, dont ever get it baked right dont mix it neither like you do. . . . He seems very happy and if I were to tell you of his cooking you would think me extravagant in my account of it. I tell you of all this to show you he is doing just his best and I think will continue to do so. He says if Uncle Davy could see me fry chicken & see my Dough Nuts he would quit talking about me coming home for him to learn me.

I do not covet your property or anyone else's. I do wish however that I had just such a Boy as Berry.

John B. Lamar to Mary Ann Cobb
Macon, June 17, 1854

I have placed Berry with Cousin Sarah to learn the mysteries of the "cuisine" which she is so competent to teach him. The Dr says Berry is making fine progress. And I think he will make me [a] good cook some of these days.

Sarah A. Rees to John B. Lamar
Americus, July 21, 1854

Berry says I must remember him to you and tell you he is fond of cooking and that he is well satisfied. He sings and whistles except when I am by, and is quite a favorite with the children.

He has not cooked as well of late and himself and kitchen I have had to complain of not being as neat as formerly. The excessive hot weather is so relaxing that I have no doubt it makes him more careless as he is young and unaccustomed to be over the fire. He has applied twice to me to visit his Father and Mother and I objected to his walking that distance at this season of the year and during such heat, and did not like his going with

---

56. John B. purchased Davy as a cook and caterer in 1850. John B. Lamar to Mary Ann Cobb, June 18, 1850.

Mr. Bivins man. I told him I should prefer his putting off until fall the visit, but it was to keep him in health that I said this.

Sarah A. Rees to John B. Lamar

Americus, [late summer 1854]

I told you Berry had become a little careless but he is young and unaccustomed to be over the fire, and the weather so intensely hot as to relax the system and I think it this instead of indifference. . . .

Shall I let him go to see his Parents when he can ride there or put it off for cooler weather.

Sarah A. Rees to John B. Lamar

Americus, November 3, 1854

[Berry] is not doing as well as he has done, growing indifferent about his cooking and *exceedingly careless* as to the neatness of his person his kitchen Towels and cooking vessels. I think it is all owing to his running about at night and he feels stupid for the want of sleep and is therefore too dull to be industrious or systomatic. Everything is put off until he shall feel like doing it and if I will not wait until then it is so badly done that I get vexed with him.

I dislike to send him to Brantly[57] as you directed but told him when you came I should call him into your presence and then tell you all as I felt it my duty to do, as you did not send him here to get bad habits but good ones to be useful & reliable and not troublesome and faithless, . . . I have had Berry called in and read this to him. He seems quite sorry says he will do better and says all I have written is so, but it shall not be so in future. . . . He is young and there are so many to draw off from duty in this wretched place that I can excuse a good deal in Berry.

Mr Hill at The Hotel wanted to whip him a few days ago for cutting off a favorite Dogs foot. Dr Rees was sent for by Dr Fish & Dr Rees would not let him whip Berry yet we all feel sorry he should have done it. He gave fifty dollars for The Dog, Fish says.

---

57. Bailey [or Balda] J. Brantley (born ca. 1805) served as the overseer on the Cobbs' Sumter County plantations. U.S. Census, 1850, Sumter County, Georgia.

Sarah A. Rees to John B. Lamar

Americus, December 18, 1854

I feel sorry to have to report to you unfavorably of Berry, he seems to be very regardless of anything I can say to him and to pay no more respect to your message sent by me to him. Dr Rees and I have told him not to leave the lot without permission from one or the other of us, and a written permit to take with him. I told him he could have this twice or thrice a week if he had attended to his duties as was his duty—if it was omitted *entirely* or *very badly done*, He should be denied the privilege of going. He goes where he pleases every night, and leaves all unattended to and keeps himself *very dirty*.

Now will you come down tomorrow with William *or* shall I send Berry to Brantley to break in and instruct him to bring him up when *he Brantley* thinks Berry will be somewhat obedient.

Dr Rees give him a little switching but it has not mortified him or caused any change for the better. If you cannot come shall I have the marshal punish him *or* send him to The Professor [Brantley] at Spring Creek. He is smart very, and very brisk and has done finely for a young inexperienced Cook. Indeed his cooking has been much praised by our Visitors and was by William this morning. He does now well, when he feels like it, this is seldom as during the day he feels the want of sleep and rest which he does not take at night.

Sarah A. Rees to John B. Lamar

Americus, January 31, 1855

As Berry is rather extravagant in his clothes, I have thought it best to say something about this to you. He had of the checks you give him seven Aprons, which he did not wear out, but quit wearing them and making lame excuses for not doing so, until I determined he should do so, and then found he had torn them up in his room to use in improper manner. I give him four pair of Summer pantaloons and three shirts. With what he brought he was well supplied, I have given him four new Aprons which had not been washed also three new shirts never washed which he has taken to Spring Creek also 5 pairs of woolen kersey pantaloons, & 2 blankets.

I have given him three hats and he brought with him a new cap. I know
not what he does with them. So I think Mr. Brantley had best put by part
of his regimentals until he gets him ready to come back.

If Mr. Brantley will make Berry obey me, I have no fear that I shall fail
to make him invaluable as a cook. He is smart has a turn for cooking and
is brisk. All he wants is to know he must do and do my way and not his. He
gets rid of his shoes too fast as well as the things mentioned.

He can now make yeast, make light bread & several kinds of bread
and biscuits although he fails oftener in these than in any other thing,
and only for the reason that he will not always make them up in time. He
makes fine Soups and cooks vegetables well and Egg Plant three ways, he
does nicely beside a good many other things that he can now do without
my being out in the kitchen. If Berry was mine and would obey me as he
did the first few months he was here it would take a large sum to buy him
from me. So just have Brantley break the young gentleman in and send
him back.

Sarah A. Rees to John B. Lamar
Americus, March 6, 1855

[Berry] did not come even to speak to me until I sent for him, he then
came and handed your note with the ten dollars enclosed, did not speak
or look at me, said I, are you sick Berry, no mam, are you cold no mam,
then began to cry, what is the matter Berry, I did not want to come from
home I done got used to the work now, and I want to stay there, why then
said I, did you not tell Cousin John this and how you were intending to
behave when you got here. He would not give me time. . . . He has not
done anything that I have told him to do and not cooked until Sunday
Dinner, I only got Supper & Breakfast, and his dinner was poor and Mon-
days Breakfast and his whole course since his return caused Dr Rees to go
& whip him, but he is still in a bad humour. I have never seen anything of
this in Berry since I have known him, for he is always happy whistling &
singing. He came back in an ill humour and keeps in it. I have him cooking. . . . The children are all fond of Berry and now out to see him and
he would not speak to them. I was never more surprised for I could not
have believed him capable of persisting in such a course eight days, *if he
could begin it*. Dr Rees says if he does not obey me & get in a better humour, he shall whip him again and give him a better one next time so as
not to leave him mad. . . .

I thought Berry would be full of joy to get back. *He wills it all otherwise* . . . said I, now what is your object Berry, what do you intend by this course. He said nothing did he intend, and that he has no object.

Sarah A. Rees to John B. Lamar
Americus, March 22, 1855

I received yours and read it to Berry and it proved effectual in bringing him out of the sulky mood yet he was indifferent as to how he did things and would not do but little of what I give him to do. Dr Rees cut a switch and used it on him and Berry then did worse.

I told him I should send for The Marshal and let him whip him as you directed and if I was forced to this he should be in a good humor before he was let off and willing to do anything I ordered and as I directed. He is now as happy as ever and is doing admirably. . . .

He is now whistling and singing and quite musical of evenings.

Sarah A. Rees to John B. Lamar
Americus, April 17, 1855

I will say this that Berry cannot be excelled in making Pea Soup, Turtle Soup, Mock Turtle, Okra, Chicken Beef and Vegetable Soups.

He cooks Meats, Breads and Vegetables *well* makes excellent Coffee & Tea. He is self willed and has become troublesome about his clothes and his kitchen vessels & towels he will not be neat enough or *careful* enough. Breakage is considerable.

"A Friend" to John B. Lamar
Sumterville, June 6, 1855

You certinley dont know how your overseer is managing. . . . Your negroes have bin whipt more this year a Ready than they have bin for 2 years past all put together. Abram & Jim Suckey has bin whipt. Abram is whipt unreasonable. Jim says Barwick will not let him attend to his hogs & if any dies which there are 40 Missing at the piney woods pen & Barwick tells Jim if he dont get the number he will whip him severe. One of the women lost a child a few days past & had it on the way home from the field. The child is ded & the woman may die yet. You have no ydea the cruel management them negroes has to under go. Your negroes are gettin a bad caracter just from Barwicks management. I wonder they dont all Run away. It is none of my Business but as a friend I wish you knew how B Manages. When you Read this Burn it.

 A Friend.

Sarah A. Rees to John B. Lamar
Americus, June 9, 1855

I must now write to tell you of Berry. He has become so fond of gambling, that he neglects everything else. A few weeks ago Bivins Negro & Berry sat up in our kitchen all night Sunday until 2 oclock Monday morning gambling. I heard a noise and got Dr Rees up to see what & where & he found them at cards in the kitchen give each of them a whipping and find that there is a sett and they alternate their meeting places but are up almost every night. The consequence is that Berry is very self willed and will send in meals sometimes in such manner that I am provoked, other times nicely served. He either gives away or sells his clothes and mortifies me to see him so dirty as he goes. He will not obey me only when *he chooses*, and thinks it too much trouble for him to clean his kitchen & cooking vessels. And I only get it done of late by carrying Dr Rees out to see the condition of things and he then orders it done by a certain time so if left undone he has sometimes given Berry a switching and it does no good, as he laughs & tells others of it and also that he had ploughed a little for Bos at The Plantation. I can assure you that notwithstanding Berry, being so brisk so apt and so healthy that he needs a tight rein to control him, six months since no one could have made me believe Berry would behave as he now does. He tells awful stories but his redeeming quality is that there is not an impudent word to me from him.

He can cook most things as well as cooks usually do, and many dishes he cannot be excelled in. I have just had Berry called in and read him this letter and asked him if it was true, Yes Miss Sarah every word except the gambling; I know I dont sit up all night at it. . . .

All the children love him and think him very wise. And they will give him anything they have and do for him. I [have] to punish Berry for not at all attending to what I told him especially must be done, locked him up on The Sabbath Day in the Dairy. Bud carried him his meals and did not know but that he was to be kept there at night & carried him bedclothes, put them in between the Slats on the window. When Dr Rees went to turn out The Prisoner found him well cared for. But Berry had taken off the Slats & stayed out whilst we were out at Church.

John T. Lamar[58] to John B. Lamar
Sumter County Plantations, July 5, 1855

I have concluded being the Physician on your Plantations to inform you that unless some "Check" is put upon your overseer . . . nearly all of your Negro Women at that place who are in the (Family Way) will loose their offspring. The overseer seems to have neither judgement or discretion, one of the women a short time since was compelled to have her child *Born* in the Field. Since that another has had one under circumstances which make me suppose, unless you "Check" him, that he will play the very "Devil." I merely write you this that you may inquire into matters. I felt it my duty to inform you.

B. J. Brantly to John B. Lamar
Sumter County Plantations, July 10, 1855

The negroes all keep well esept Nancy Florida. She is vary sick an I am afraid that she will mak a dye of it. The doctor says she has got dropsey of the chest. He is attending on her twice a day. I feel uneasy about the old lady myself.

Stancil Barwick to John B. Lamar
Sumter County Plantations, July 13, 1855

I riceve your letter on yesterday Eving. Was vary sorry to hear that you had heard that I was treating your Negroes so cruely. Now sir I do say to you in truth that the report is false. Thear is no trauth in it. No man nor set of men has Ever seen me misstreat one of the Negroes on the Place. Now as

---

58. John T. Lamar was a cousin and physician in Americus.

regards the wimin loosing children treaty lost one it is true. I never heard
of her being in that way untill she lost it. She was at the house all time. I
never made her doo any work at all. She said to me . . . that she did not
no that she was in that way her self untill she lost the child. As regards Li-
uzianer she was in the field it is true but she workt as she Please. I never
said a word to hear in any way at all untill she com to me in the field an
said that she was sick. I told hear to go home. She started an on the way
she misscarrid. She was a bout five months gone. This is the true stat-
ment of case. Now sir apon my word an hounor I hav tride to carry out
your wishis as near as I posibly could doo. . . . Reports that has reacht you
must hav been carrid from this Place by Negroes. . . . Two or three hard
cases . . . I hav had to Deal with Ruff but not cruely at all. Among them
Abram has been as triflin as any man on the Place.

Sarah A. Rees to John B. Lamar

Americus, July 21, 1855

Notwithstanding your not replying to my letters, I have concluded to do
what I believe to be right in regard not only to *you*, but to *myself* and also
to *Berry*. . . .

Can you not come down for a few days before you go North it may
prove the salvation of Berry here and hereafter. I think it important
Cousin John; I write you this so that Berry may not be ruined but made
valuable.

Joe E. Wells to John B. Lamar

Macon, August 31, 1855

Louisa got a letter from Sumter saying . . . that Berry's Mother was dead.

Sarah A. Rees to John B. Lamar

Americus, November 8, 1855

I am sorry to tell you that I had to have The Marshal to whip Berry about
two weeks ago, sent for him to repeat it this morning, and Berry ran
off. I suppose he will be taken care of by The Negroes at some of your

places. . . . I think if The Overseer will punish him well and bring him back tied this may mortify him and convince him he cannot have his own way altogether and that he has not set either yourself or myself at defiance.

Sarah A. Rees to John B. Lamar
Americus, May 21, 1856

I well know that you are angry at me, and I cannot imagine what way I offended. I did more with Berry than I would for any other Persons Servant . . . I bore with Berry for two other reasons one, that I felt that as you had given Sis so elegant a Piano I would do all I possibly could to not only make a cook of Berry but to keep him from bad habits & c. . . . I should not have sent for A Marshal if you had not told me to do it if he persisted in going without permission. He would promise me to do better and this or that should not be so again and would do the same day after day.

John A. Cobb II to John B. Lamar
Athens, May 12, 1857

Lamar whiped Alfred yesterday for lending out his saddle and in the evening when we came home he could not be found and we have heard nothing of him since, just at this time his absence puts everything out of place.

Mary Ann Cobb to Howell Cobb
Athens, July 10, 1857

John[59] takes the entire control of larder, servants, grounds & stables, and the servants like him, still they stand in awe of him more than they ever did of you or me. He is kind and accessible, and if anything goes awry the elders do not fear to approach him and make explanation, but if the younger try, from Alfred down do not obey his orders strictly, he will

---

59. John A. Cobb II.

bring them to an account. He has had troublesome circumstances to arise during the first few months, and but for John's shrewdness, and tenacity, this mischief would have gone on increasing, but he has got the youngsters on our lot to believe they cannot do anything "Mas. Johnny" cannot find out, and "I'm afraid Mas. Johnny will whip me," keeps them from lying and stealing, when the ten commandments would have [no] effect. Alfred *ran* away soon after you left and Lucius has been making accts at the cake & candy shop. Rachel does not want to go to the plantation. Sylvia was unhappy for awhile but seems *resigned* to her fate, her girls likewise. I suppose they think the marriage market at Washington unfavorable to their hopes. Everything is deranged about the house. No system in housekeeping and everything and everybody is *mixed up* so that there is no head or foot, no mistress or maid, all on a footing looking out daily for the final breaking up, that will bring things to a settlement. I am *ready* and *willing* to be disenthralled, and disenfranchised I may say.

John B. Lamar to John A. Cobb II

Sumter County Plantations, November 17, 1857

That interesting representative of coloured society, Alfred has become disgusted with rural life & turned his face again toward the polished ebony circles of Athens. I sent him down on the cars yesterday was a week, to stay with his parents at Barwicks until Rhodes came by, to settle the new plantation in Worth—the young man concluded yesterday as the waggons & negroes were leaving, not to go with them.

I write to request you, as soon as you get this to see Capt Dorsey & tell him if he will be on the look out for the gentleman on his arrival, & put him in jail, I will pay him *twenty dollars*. If the Capt succeeds in taking him & putting him in jail, I wish you to furnish him with warm clothes & plenty of blankets & let him remain comfortably under the paternal care of the jailer until I send for him—which will not be in a hurry. Solitary confinement on jail fare is the best prescription I can think of for his case big-head. He left without the slightest cause, except disgust with country life, as Rhodes had never seen him & Barwick had taken no control over [him] during the week he was at the plantation. His example will have a bad effect on the other negroes, until he is punished for his conduct, and my plan is to let him stay in jail awhile.

John B. Lamar to John A. Cobb II

Macon, November 25, 1857

I wrote you from Sumter & sent the letter by the waggoner to mail at Americus. . . . I write again to tell you that, that interesting young man Alfred has ran away before Rhodes (the Worth overseer) even laid eyes on him. Please get Capt Dorsey to take him up & put him in jail in Watkinsville & I will pay him twenty dollars for his trouble.

He will probably be about the lot of Mrs. Taylor where I understand he has a mistress.

If he is caught & lodged in jail, furnish him with warm clothing & blankets so that he will be comfortable & let him remain until I send for him.

John A. Cobb II to John B. Lamar

Athens, November 30, [1857]

Alfred came to me about 7 oclock saturday night . . . & this morning I have . . . given him to Moon to take him to Watkinsville & by 12 oclock he will be in jail to await your orders. . . .

His idea for coming up here was that I would hire him out, *A bright Idea.* He brought nearly all of the clothing that he had with him, I have given him (4) four good Blankets & I think with that he can keep himself *warm.*

John A. Cobb II to John B. Lamar

Athens, December 4, 1857

I wrote to Lamar the other day & I told him about Alfred therefore I did not write to you. I had him tied & he got away from me & Moon & myself went after him & Moon found him in Mrs. Maxwells stable. We then tied him & carried him to Watkinsville & put him in jail were he is now. I think that Moon is entitled to the $20.

Joseph T. Rhodes to John B. Lamar
Worth Place Plantation, January 10, 1858

We have a very strang kind of fever here it comes with a sore throat and swells the jaws like the mumps and ends with the worst cough ever, felt worse than the whooping cough. . . . I am cuting down my swamp as fast as I can.

T. H. Gibson to John B. Lamar
Dahlonega, January 16, 1858

A runaway negro Boy was captured By James N. Jones M. V. Worley Henry Davis & C. W. Worley who calls his Name Ed, and says he belongs to John B Lamar of Macon, that he ran away from Charles Rhoes an overseer of Worth County, he is now in Jail at this place you will please come & Take him if he has stated falsely Please inform me as I dont desire by advertisement to run the owner to unnecessary Expense.

Samuel Stephens to John B. Lamar
[Near Dahlonega], January 16, 1858

S. B. Barker W. C. Cole James M. Welchel and myself hav caught a negro man who says his name is Edward and left your plantation in Worth County, Ga because of abuse of your overseer, Charles Roads. We followed him a distance of twenty miles was joined by Messors Worleys Davis & Jones of Dahlonega caught him without injury and put him in Jail at Dahlonega on the 15th inst. He is in fine health. Said boy is of dark complexion about 5 feet 10 in high quick spokin well dressed and we think about 25 years old.

  If he is yours you will pleas write at your earlyest convinience pay expence and take him away as if you disir it we will bring him home by your paying expence & c.

W. C. Cole to Howell Cobb

[Near Dahlonega], January 18, 1858

Stephens & myself with others caught a Negro man on Saturday the 16 inst after a chase of some 24 miles with a Pack of Negro Dogs. We Lodged the Boy in our Jail at Dahlonega Geo until we find his ownr.

Said Boy says that his name is Edward and Belongs to John B Lamar of *Macon, Ga.* I Sand a Negro man from Athens Tells me that the Boy Belongs to you that he is your Carrige Drive and that his Name is *Alfred.* The Boy from Athens further says that Said Boy was sent to your Plantation By his mistress Mrs Cobb and after a fiw days he fell out with annothe Negro and killed him that this Boy Runaway and was caut and put in Jail and from this he had made his escape.

This Boy is likely and is about 5 ft-10 about 23 or 25 years old Small Hands and Feet and 2 or 3 small scars on his fase, verry Pert Spoken and verry Smart. He has evry appearance of Being a House Boy and Not a Field Hand. If he is your Boy and is guilty of the above crime if you wish I will attend to the matter for you By you sending me a Bill of Sale I will take him to New Orleans and dispose of him at Short Notice. I have written to John B Lamar Esq for information whether he is his owner or not.

Said Boy Says his intention was to Reach a Free State—he gave us a chase of 12 hours and must of Run at Least 50 miles in the Rout. We started him at Leathrs ford at the Line of Hall and Lumpkin Co . . . and caught him on the Blue Ridge a distance of 24 miles Strate Line—if you desire my assistance I will settle with those that assisted in the arrest and Jail Expenses & c.

John B. Lamar to John A. Cobb II

Macon, January 20, 1858

Alfred (or as he calls himself in that latitude Edward) is in jail in Dahlonega, after a chase of 20 miles so I learn from T H Gibson jailor at Dahlonega & also from Saml Stephens. . . .

I have written to both—that I will give *fifty dollars*, all expenses included except jail fees—for his delivery to the jail in Macon. And that whoever brings him, can call on you on the way down for 20$ of the money to pay expenses to Macon. If you pay the 20$ write me immediately, so that I may know what to pay when the man comes with Alfred.

Dont pay the money to anyone unless he has Alfred, as there are several who were in the chase & the wrong man may call. Whoever has Alfred will be the right man of course.

Howell Cobb to John B. Lamar
Washington, D.C., January 24, 1858

Enclosed I send you a letter I got by the last mail. I know nothing of the writer, but I have no doubt it is Alfred to whom he alludes. I suppose the killing of a negro is all a made up affair. Would it not be well enough to send Alfred off & sell him? He will never do for a house servant & would be an injury on the plantation. I think, if you can get a trusty man to undertake it, I would send him to New Orleans & dispose of him.

W. C. Cole to John B. Lamar
[Near Dahlonega], January 25, 1858

Yours of the 20th inst is recd and in Reply can safely say that it is your Boy that wee caught.

I called to see Mr A. B. Barker who is the owner of the dogs that wee followed your Boy with, and who keeps a Pack for the express Business of ketching Runaways. I showed him your letter, he says in reply that he with others ought to have $30 for putting said Boy in Jail as their was 14 in company and Run that Boy at Least 50 miles a chase of 12 hours we started the Boy at the line of Hall County and caught him at the Blue Ridge at Coopers Gap But our srvases was volunteerd theirfore wee leave it with you to Pay us as you feel disposed I would now Bring you the Boy at your offer But for the Reason that the Jail fees and the expense of myself and Boy to Macon & my expenses Back Would not Be less than about 38 or 40 and the Boys would look to me for about 30 to Be divided as wee all Had to Be out expenses of supper and Horse feed at the Hotel at Dahlonega and then 12 oclock at nite Before wee Reached Home

But I will deliver your Boy to John A Cobb or Thos Cobb or Capt W. H. Dorsey or at Watkinsville Jail for $65 and I will pay all expenses Whitch will be about 15 days Jail fees Besides the 30 to Be divided

The fact is the Boy is a smart Rascal and must Be Jailed every Nite and Handcufft during the day and a eye on him all the time.

He is a sounde fellow and can fite dogs with a vengeance. . . .

NB. I had adrressed Hon H Cobb as the day after wee wrote you wee lrnd that alfred Belonged to him No answer as yet.

Our chase was in the goldmines and mountains not in the Piny Woods.

Samuel Stephens to John B. Lamar

[Near Dahlonega], January 26, 1858

Your letter of 20 came to hand and was as I am informed answered by W. C. Cole in my absence. From your letter I have no doubt but the boy we lodged in jail is the boy Alford you have described. I am informed that T. H. Gibson has taken said boy without our knowledge and started to Macon with him. We hope he will arive safe but cannot vouch for him as we know nothing about how said boy is confined. Mr. Gibson has taken said boy on his own responsibility having been appointed jailer by the Inferior court of Lumpkin county. He had nothing to do with the arest of said boy Alfred and we feel ourselves entitled to whatever reward you may pleas to pay as we was at considerable trouble. As liberal a reward as the circumstances will justify will be thankfully recieved. We are pleged to some of our party for servises rendered in the arest. You will pleas remit the same to us.

Joseph T. Rhodes to John B. Lamar

Worth Place Plantation, August 1, 1858

I have a negro *Izeal* runaway. He left last saterday week. I have not heard from him yet. I guess he is about macon. I was whiping one of his boys about stealing Rosting ears and he came runing up to where I was and told me to quit the boy was not guilty so I run in with him with my fist having nothing else. I knocked him Down. He arose and left cursing.

Lamar Cobb to John B. Lamar

Washington, D.C., November 17, 1858

While I was in Macon one of the negroes from Baldwin, Antony by name, came over to your house, his legs were swollen a little so I let him remain two or three days for him to recover & then gave him a pass & sent him back to the plantation with a note to Goodson stating my having kept him in Macon for two or three days, but I said *nothing* at all in regard to his whipping him or his having run away. Was I *right* in so doing?

CHAPTER 4

"I Hope You Will Not Think
That I Am Ungratful"

SPRING COMES EARLY AND FAST IN Athens, Georgia. The month of April often feels like May or June in places farther north, in climates more gentle. The processes of creation and destruction are on full, beautiful, heartless display in the Georgia Piedmont, and the soil pulses with the energy of life urgently pushing itself into being. Grasses and shrubs and trees erupt into vibrant bloom, snakes wake up hungry and active from their winter stupor, and a sickly yellow coating of pine pollen covers everything.

For the Cobb children, spring 1842 was likely a glorious opportunity to shed their winter wool, relish open windows and warm breezes, and begin playing outside. Mary Ann spent that spring concerning herself with the onerous task of compiling a detailed inventory of all her family's possessions and the less burdensome thoughts of Easter finery. Yet for fifteen-year-old Aggy Carter and her family, spring 1842 must have left them feeling like they were standing at the gates of hell. On the morning of April 7, amid blooming formal gardens and snakes in the grass, both proverbial and real, she, her parents, and her siblings stood silently on the front porch of the Cobb mansion and waited to be sold.

The Carters most likely were told that their public auction, along with that of beautiful furniture, was necessary to cover the debts of the bankrupt Cobb family. They likely were told that their loyalty over the preceding years all but ensured that they would be saved from the worst possible outcomes, if the Cobbs could even have appreciated what those worst possible outcomes might have been. They likely were told to be patient and behave. But all the guises of paternalism and the imagined bonds of affection fell to ash when human beings were forced to stand on a grand front porch of an exquisite hilltop mansion. Then they had to accept that the people they had known and served for a lifetime had the power and

the intention to sell them along with other pieces of valuable but ultimately disposable property.

Aggy and her family were no doubt terrified that April morning. They
had witnessed the horror of the sale and permanent separation in the
lives of other enslaved people, but now it was happening to them. One
can barely begin to imagine their heart-rending anguish, their fear, their
sense of utter betrayal and bewilderment that it had all come to this. Being forced to stand on the porch and await the auctioneer's hammer
made stunningly clear that neither faithful service nor human connections that had been forged through years of close proximity could guarantee the sanctity of their family. There may once have been days when
it was possible to believe that they were all in it together, but the early
weeks of the spring of 1842 exploded that myth once and for all. It had
always been about the Cobbs and what they wanted, what they needed.
What they needed now was money, even more than they wanted to protect the people they had owned and relied on for years. Their continued
affluence depended on their ability to ignore the humanity of those they
enslaved and treat them instead as saleable property.[1] The invisible scars
of this cold calculus would shape the lives of all involved for decades to
come.

While no record of the events of April 7 survive, it appears likely that
Aggy's world was ripped apart that day. Her mother, Silva, and her sisters, Polly and Eliza, were sold.[2] The Cobbs, for their part, were clearly
stressed over the potential loss of the entire family and plotted ways to
keep at least some of them from being offered at a second sale. Sarah
Rootes Cobb wrote to her daughter-in-law, "I felt for all the negroes, but
for [Aggy], I did keenly feel as I never could reconcile it to myself for her
or her brothers or sisters to be sold if it could by any lawful means be pre-

---

1. Historian Walter Johnson wrote of the intellectual machinations that were necessary
for, in his phrase, "turning people into prices." Walter Johnson, *Soul by Soul: Life Inside the
Antebellum Slave Market* (Cambridge: Harvard University Press, 2003), 18. See also Daina
Ramey Berry, *The Price of Their Pound of Flesh* (Boston: Beacon Press, 2017); and James Oakes,
Slavery and Freedom: An Interpretation of the Old South (New York: W. W. Norton & Company,
1990), 21–24.

2. See chapter 2, note 10. While Aggy's mother and sister Polly do not appear in any
Cobb-Lamar document after March 1842, the same is not true for her sister Eliza. Eliza, who
in this case is specifically identified as Aggy's sister, is mentioned in an 1869 letter written by
Samuel Cobb, whom the family had previously enslaved. There is no evidence, however, that
there had been any contact between Aggy and her sister over the preceding twenty-seven
years. Samuel Cobb to Mary Ann Cobb, October 5, 1869.

vented."[3] It could not. In October 1843, the remaining family members again endured public auction. Once more they stood on the front porch of the mansion where they had served for years, among the fine furniture and drapery, above the grass where they had spent countless days watching the Cobb boys play, and listened to the chant of the auctioneer. The sale went through. Unknown buyers bought Aggy's brothers Nelson and Ellick. John B. purchased Aggy, Mary Ann's most valued servant, and returned her to his sister. He also purchased Aggy's father, George, and her brother Robert. While George remained with the Cobbs, John B. carried Robert to Macon and had him trained as a wheelwright. Aggy's life was valued at $400.[4]

Aggy and George were the only two of eight members of their family who moved to the Cowpens Plantation with the Cobbs that winter. There they joined Bob, who had spent a lifetime laboring for the Cobbs and was now simply hoping for a wig to cover his aging head, and the roughly one dozen house servants who were brought there after surviving the preceding two brutal years.

In the hallways of the Cowpens house, Aggy joined an unfortunate-but-select group of individuals who had learned to work the system to their advantage. All had weathered the vicissitudes of the Cobbs' financial turmoil, even though some of their family members had not. She and George arrived there especially wounded. He had labored to make himself invaluable to the Cobbs. He had proven himself worthy, along with Bob, to be one of their two most trusted couriers. He likely had spent years teaching his children that their family's experience of slavery was different, perhaps gentler, than they saw for others because he had repeatedly demonstrated his loyalty to the family. Then he was forced to stand for sale, twice.

George must have been gutted by the sale of his wife and children. Yet he also must have been a master at swallowing his grief and concealing his frustrations. Otherwise he never would have found himself at the Cowpens immediately following the devastation of the sale. Cloistered

---

3. Sarah Rootes Cobb to Mary Ann Cobb, undated [1842–43]. The *Southern Whig* (Athens) listed Aggy's parents, George and Silva, as well as their children Aggy, Robert, Polly, and Eliza for sale in the spring of 1842. *Southern Whig*, March 18, 1842. The following year, the newspaper advertised a second opportunity to purchase George, as well as his remaining children, Nelson, Aggy, Ellick, and Robert. *Southern Banner* (Athens), September 7, 1843; *Southern Whig*, September 16, 1843.

4. Aggy Carter bill of sale, James Hendon to John B. Lamar, October 21, 1843.

there with those who enslaved him, holding himself together in the face of unbearable loss, he must have been a perfect model of how to put the desire to survive into action. If he had been teaching these lessons to his children for years, they became all the more urgent for his daughter during that winter of their despair. The knowledge of how to survive the system, rather than overtly resist it, became the most valuable thing he could give her. The lessons he imparted to her there, drawn from the depths of his grief, shaped the ways she lived the remainder of her life in slavery.

Aggy learned her father's lessons well. Howell's younger sister, Mary Willis, had taught her to read and write in the early 1830s. This relatively unique skill among the enslaved gave her an important tool for demonstrating her value to the family.[5] So too did her intimate connection with the Cobb children. Aggy began working as a nursemaid following the birth of Mary Ann's first child in 1836, when she was herself still a small girl of about nine. By the time they arrived at the Cowpens in late 1843, still reeling from the losses of the preceding two years and searching for a way to guarantee her future security, she consciously labored to present herself as the most consistently trustworthy servant Mary Ann ever had.

When Howell and Mary Ann left the Cowpens for Washington that year, Sarah Rootes Cobb wrote that they need not worry about their sons. "I keep Aggy with them constantly," she explained with confidence, "and she appears very careful of them."[6] Sarah marveled, too, that Aggy was "very zealous" in teaching the boys their alphabet.[7] The Cobb children loved Aggy, and she returned the affection in kind. Several years later, when the children were traveling with Mary Ann, Aggy wrote asking that she "ples remember [me] kindly to all of the littel ladys and the tow littel jenttelmen. I miss them very much but I hope tha ma hav a nice time in macon."[8]

As the children outgrew the need for a playmate and babysitter, or even a nursemaid who could teach them their letters, Aggy continued to re-

---

5. On the children of slaveholding families teaching the enslaved to read, see Wilma King, *Stolen Childhood: Slave Youth in Nineteenth-Century America*, rev. ed. (Bloomington: Indiana University Press, 2011), 181–82; and Elizabeth Fox-Genovese, *Within the Plantation Household: Black and White Women of the Old Plantation South* (Chapel Hill: University of North Carolina Press, 1988), 156.

6. Sarah Rootes Cobb to Mary Ann Cobb, February 18, 1844.

7. Sarah Rootes Cobb to Mary Ann Cobb, January 5, 1845.

8. Aggy Mills to Mary Ann Cobb, January 13, [1862].

make herself to remain integral to their upbringing.[9] She turned a careful eye toward the etiquette and manners required of polite society and perfected the roles to the extent that she could teach them to the Cobb children. When the Cobb daughters were invited to a party, Mary Ann reported that she did not concern herself with ensuring that the girls would make a good public impression. "*Aggy's* dressing them," she wrote, "and will go with them [to] see that they behave and such *proper* things."[10]

Aggy's careful attention to the Cobb children allowed her to weave herself into Mary Ann's trust. Her affection for them also came at the point at which she was beginning to think about a family of her own. Yet having lived in forced exile from her mother and siblings, she understood the potential risks of marriage and family for an enslaved woman.[11] When de-

---

9. As numerous scholars have pointed out, there is nothing unusual about an eight- or nine-year-old enslaved girl being brought into her owner's household to care for their children. Most agree, however, that such an experience was not a training ground for a lifetime of domestic service and that most enslaved girls were equally likely to be sent back to the fields or into other forms of service as the white children matured. As Sylvia's story makes clear, this seems to have been how the Cobb-Lamars understood the process. It is not Aggy's arrival in the household as a nine-year-old girl that is remarkable but rather her ability to continue to educate herself as she and the Cobb children grew so that she was retained beyond the point at which others might have been dismissed. Scholarship on enslaved children as nursemaids does not appear to contain many examples of those children being trusted as teachers when the white children were of the age to learn to read and write, and even fewer of them being entrusted as teenagers to help their charges perfect the type of manners needed both in the household and out in proper society. See Fox-Genovese, *Within the Plantation Household*, 147, 152–56. See also Anthony E. Kaye, *Joining Places: Slave Neighborhoods of the Old South* (Chapel Hill: University of North Carolina Press, 2007), 86, 89; Erskine Clarke, *Dwelling Place: A Plantation Epic* (New Haven: Yale University Press, 2005), 19, 31, 58; and Stephanie M. H. Camp, *Closer to Freedom: Enslaved Women and Everyday Resistance in the Plantation South* (Chapel Hill: University of North Carolina Press, 2004), 32.

10. Mary Ann Cobb to Howell Cobb Jr., May 13, 1859.

11. On courtship and the risks of marriage for the enslaved, see Rebecca J. Fraser, *Courtship and Love among the Enslaved in North Carolina* (Jackson: University Press of Mississippi, 2007); Emily West, *Chains of Love: Slave Couples in Antebellum South Carolina* (Urbana: University of Illinois Press, 2004), 43–74. See also Tera W. Hunter, *Bound in Wedlock: Slave and Free Black Marriage in the Nineteenth Century* (Cambridge: Belknap Press of Harvard University Press, 2017), 23–24, 29–31, 41–44; Daina Ramey Berry, *Swing the Sickle for the Harvest Is Ripe: Gender and Slavery in Antebellum Georgia* (Champaign: University of Illinois Press, 2007), 58–59; Cynthia Kennedy, *Braided Relations, Entwined Lives: The Women of Charleston's Urban Slave Society* (Bloomington: Indiana University Press, 2005), 96–100; Kaye, *Joining Places*, 51–54; Rebecca J. Griffin, "'Goin' Back over There to See That Girl': Competing Social Spaces in the Lives of the Enslaved in Antebellum North Carolina," *Slavery and Abolition* 25, no. 1 (April 2004): 94–113; Dylan C. Penningroth, *The Claims of Kinfolk: African American Property and Community in the Nineteenth-Century South* (Chapel Hill: University of North Carolina Press, 2003), 103–7; Herbert Gutman, *The Black Family in Slavery and Freedom, 1750–1925* (New York: Vintage Books, 1976), 11–28, 70–75.

ciding to pursue a relationship, Aggy elected to conduct her romance in ways that she knew Mary Ann would find reassuring.

By the winter of 1849, she had begun a courtship with Isaac Mills, the body servant and "favorite negro" of the Cobbs' Athens neighbor, General Robert Taylor.[12] Aggy and Isaac would have known each other for years as they prayed together at the First Baptist Church and socialized in their free time within the small circle of local enslaved people.[13] Mary Ann recorded that at Christmas that year, Aggy spent the day with her new "beaux" after he and his fellow enslaved musicians serenaded the Cobb children.[14] Mary Ann approved the courtship and described Isaac as "a good looking mulato boy of good character" and a suitable match for Aggy.[15] General Taylor, after all, was the largest slaveholder in Athens and one of the only men in town who equaled the Cobbs in wealth and position. Much like the Cobb-Lamars, his cotton empire spanned six plantations across the state.[16]

Aggy recognized that Mary Ann wanted to play a central role in the public aspects of her courtship. She and Isaac allowed their relationship to play out in full view of their masters as a way of demonstrating their trustworthiness. Within a matter of months, Mary Ann began anticipating a wedding and lamented, "I will have to supply her place with someone who can sleep in my room, particularly in the event of her marrying, which she will probably do when Maj. Taylor allows his servant to marry."[17] Isaac secured Taylor's permission and approached the Cobbs in September 1850 to ask for their consent to the union.[18] Howell "cheerfully" assented, and Mary Ann took charge of Aggy's wedding.[19]

While records exist for other, smaller weddings of the enslaved in Ath-

---

12. "The Last Will and Testament of Robert Taylor," 1853, Clarke County Courthouse Records Room, Clarke County, Georgia.

13. Both Mary Ann and General Taylor's wife were members of First Baptist Church in Athens. Aggy and Isaac attended with their mistresses and were baptized there during the Civil War. Minutes of the First Baptist Church of Athens, Georgia.

14. Mary Ann Cobb to Howell Cobb, December 25, 1849.

15. Mary Ann Cobb to Howell Cobb, September 2, 1850.

16. While Taylor's papers might have provided an opportunity to see Isaac and Aggy's lives from a different perspective, or to understand how the Cobbs' neighbor ran his own distant plantations, there is no surviving archive pertaining to his life or business.

17. Mary Ann Cobb to Howell Cobb, March 26, 1850. Mary Ann mistakenly referred here to Taylor by his rank in the Georgia Militia prior to his promotion to brigadier general in 1841. For details of his promotion, see Catherine Ann Rushing, "Balancing Roles: An Interpretation of the Taylor-Grady House," (master's thesis, University of Georgia, 2014), 11.

18. Mary Ann Cobb to Howell Cobb, September 2, 1850.

19. Howell Cobb to Mary Ann Cobb, September 6, 1850.

ens's black churches, Aggy's nuptials were no ordinary affair. Indeed, her union with Isaac provided both an occasion for celebration and an opportunity to reaffirm the Cobbs' social standing. Mary Ann constructed a party at her home for two hundred guests, black and white, to display her wealth and power. It was a grand stage on which she could publicly perform the role of a benevolent mistress sparing no expense to celebrate the love and union of her most favored chattel.[20]

Aggy reciprocated, in turn, by continuing to privately perform her role with deference and affection. Her continued success as nursemaid, companion, and confidante is evident in Mary Ann's assertion: "There is no other servant I can trust so entirely with my children."[21] The subsequent birth of Aggy's own children only served to reinforce her awareness of the importance of cultivating Mary Ann's goodwill. She and Isaac celebrated the arrival of baby Louisa "Lou" Mills, their first child, on July 18, 1851. Their second child, daughter Frances "Fanny" Mills, whom Aggy described as "the faatest colord baby I ever saw," was born several years later.[22] Yet the requirement that she accompany the Cobbs across Georgia and to Washington, D.C., disrupted her role as wife and mother. Indeed, at one point the demands on Aggy's time proved so great that the Cobbs engaged another enslaved woman to serve as a wet nurse for Louisa.

Fanny and Louisa increased the stakes for their parents, who, like all enslaved parents, now needed to protect their children as well as themselves. Aggy attempted to earn Mary Ann's favor for her toddlers, even when they were too young to do it for themselves. After the Cobbs sent her a gift from Washington, D.C., she wrote in response, "oh I do wish it was in my power to rite how gratful and thankful I am to you and I hope the lord

---

20. Mary Ann's efforts are in line with the argument of historian Simon Gikandi, who suggests that elite women used the presentation of their well-mannered and well-managed enslaved to demonstrate the extent of their own refinement and culture. Simon Gikandi, *Slavery and the Culture of Taste* (Princeton: Princeton University Press, 2011), 55–58. On weddings for the enslaved, see Hunter, *Bound in Wedlock*, 45–60; Patrick W. O'Neil, "Bosses and Broomsticks: Ritual and Authority in Antebellum Slave Weddings," *Journal of Southern History* 75, no. 1 (February 2009): 29–48; Berry, *Swing the Sickle for the Harvest Is Ripe*, 55–57; Clarke, *Dwelling Place*, 321; Kaye, *Joining Places*, 64–74; West, *Chains of Love*, 20–34; Thomas E. Will, "Weddings on Contested Grounds: Slave Marriage in the Antebellum South," *Historian* 62 (September 1999): 99–117; Ann Patton Malone, *Sweet Chariot: Slave Family and Household Structure in Nineteenth-Century Louisiana* (Chapel Hill: University of North Carolina Press, 1992), 166–79; Deborah Gray-White, *Ar'n't I a Woman: Female Slaves in the Plantation South*, rev. ed (New York: Norton & Norton, 1999), 98–99; Charles Joiner, *Down by the Riverside: A South Carolina Slave Community* (Urbana: University of Illinois Press, 1984), 136–38.

21. Mary Ann Cobb to Laura Cobb Rutherford, August 11, 1852.

22. Aggy Mills to Howell Cobb Jr., November 2, [1857].

well spar me long ornuf to rase my childran to feel the same." She simultaneously strove to instill in her daughters the need to demonstrate their appreciation and loyalty: "L[ouisa] j[oins] me in menny thanks to you and
frances wod too if she new her duty."[23] Such efforts, she hoped, would protect their place in the Cobb household. Still haunted by the memory of
that April morning a scant decade earlier, she knew that she had to do all
in her power to preserve her children should it ever happen again.

Aggy's ability to read and write allowed her to perform loyalty in ways
that even her father never could. Literacy offered her the opportunity to
reinforce her connection with Mary Ann from afar, writing to her, "I intend to cary oute all of your ordorous just as if you was hear yourself."[24]
She supervised the other enslaved members of the household, reported
back on their progress, and relayed questions related to their tasks. "Unkel Ben," she wrote from Athens, "is very bisay preparing the ground for
planting. He wants to know if you wants the barly path by the stable to
stand for seed or must he plant it in corn."[25] Her reports extended to the
spiritual life of the household, as well, evident in her note that "ant vica
and myself gos to charch on fast days and fest on prar and not cake."[26]

The Cobbs appreciated the benefits of this arrangement, with Mary
Ann proudly noting to Howell that "I had a letter from Aggy last week,
all on our lot are well & all coming on smoothly."[27] Yet there were cracks
in the edifice; the "feast" that Aggy was enjoying was not necessarily the
one the Cobbs expected. As the nation slid toward civil war, some of Athens's black churches began to question the legitimacy of the legal and
moral structures upholding slavery. African American preacher Joseph
Williams recollected in 1866 that, during his tenure in Athens, from the
late 1850s on, he had been driven by the belief that "my bible contains a
bill of right from heaven which make me free my children free & which
proclaim this birthright to every human being."[28] While there is no evidence that he preached these ideas in his public sermons, it seems likely

---

23. Aggy Mills to "My dar little misstrs," March [1857]. For enslaved parents teaching
their children how to navigate interactions with their enslavers, see King, *Stolen Childhood*,
172–75.

24. Aggy Mills to Mary Ann Cobb, January 13, [1862].

25. Aggy Mills to Mary Ann Cobb, March 11, [1862].

26. Aggy Mills to Mary Ann Cobb, March 13, [1862].

27. Mary Ann Cobb to Howell Cobb, March 20, 1862.

28. Rev. Joseph Williams to Rev. E. P. Smith, September 1, 1866, field letters of the American Missionary Association, Amistad Research Center, New Orleans (microfilm, University
of Georgia Libraries).

that as the war progressed he and members of the enslaved community began to privately discuss the prospects of freedom. Aggy likely kept her opinions on these ideas to herself but could not have ignored the pressures in the Cobb household following the election of Abraham Lincoln and Howell's resignation from his position in the Buchanan administration in protest.

During the Civil War's first two years, life changed little for most of the people enslaved by the Cobb-Lamars. While some men traveled to far-off battlefields as body servants for white family members serving in the Confederate armies, most of the enslaved continued life much as they had before the war began. This relative stability evaporated as Union forces seized portions of the coastal region, and the armies commanded by General William Tecumseh Sherman drew ever nearer to Atlanta. Confronted with the possibility of federal raids on Athens, Howell and Mary Ann expended considerable ink in their efforts to identify a safe haven to which the family might retreat. Howell counseled Mary Ann to join him at his headquarters in Macon. Following the fall of Atlanta, however, she and the children fled to the family's house in Americus. They left Aggy to watch over their Athens home and the few enslaved people they left behind.

Despite needing Aggy more than ever, Howell and Mary Ann had to confront the crumbling of their own paternalistic facade. Mary Ann ensured the safety of her children but proved willing to hazard the well-being of their nursemaid. She confided to Howell, "Poor Aggy, it hurts me to have to leave her here not knowing what her fate may be if the Yankees overrun this upcountry. She may be starved to death, or dragged to the North."[29]

Ultimately Sherman's forces took their retribution by burning the family's Hurricane Plantation in Baldwin County. The Athens house remained unscathed. Aggy suffered neither starvation nor abduction, and the war ended with her and her family continuing to serve the Cobbs as they always had. Yet even in her transition to freedom, Aggy continued to express loyalty to Mary Ann, vowing to "do just as she used to do."[30] Isaac did the same, performing day labor for the Taylors and Cobbs. However, freedom and the new spaces associated with it altered the dynamic between Aggy and her former owners.

---

29. Mary Ann Cobb to Howell Cobb, undated [Fall 1864].
30. Mary Ann Cobb to Howell Cobb, January 17, 1866.

Perhaps the first and most shocking change appeared in connection with Aggy's literacy. Her letters during the decades of her enslavement were functionally literate but rife with phonetic spellings and grammatical errors. Mary Ann appears to have proudly welcomed this as the best that was possible from a minimally educated enslaved woman. As the echoes of war faded, however, Aggy's literacy skills manifested considerable improvement. A letter from the spring of 1865 gives evidence of this new, clear, and powerful voice, as Aggy penned Mary Ann, "I am very glad to hear that you are coming home this summer. We all wish to see you very much. I am planting both gardens and if you have any particular directions to send you can let me know as I have just commenced planting. . . . We are all tolerable well. The children has had the measles and I am afraid that they are taking the whooping cough."[31] While the words convey the same message of fidelity that Aggy had always communicated in her letters, the near-perfect grammar and handwriting reveal the extent to which she had carefully concealed the breadth of her education.

Mary Ann was an astute observer of her world. She had read decades of Aggy's notes and believed that they reflected the full extent of her literacy. Mary Ann must have recognized the remarkable change in Aggy's means of communication and its implications. As the world of the slaveholding South crumbled around her, so too did her surety of Aggy's straightforward loyalty. The March 1865 letter must have raised a profound question. Had Aggy been her closest ally and confidante, or had she been performing a role for nearly thirty years? Mary Ann believed the latter. In the aftermath of this shattering realization, she came to view Aggy through the same prism of distrust that had defined her previous judgments of Sylvia and Rachel. While she could not threaten to banish the freedwoman to the plantation, as she had with the others, she now had the option to simply dismiss her. Howell advised against it, however, and counseled, "I doubt you will be able to do as well. It will be difficult to get good servants for the next year." He suggested that the old order with Aggy and Isaac would be restored "when freedom has had its day, and the negroes have learned from experience what it is to be free."[32]

The situation did not improve. Aggy's decision to abruptly reveal the extent of her literacy might have been an attempt to begin shaking off the affectations that had shaped the preceding three decades of her life.

---

31. Aggy Mills to Mary Ann Cobb, March 7, 1865.
32. Howell Cobb to Mary Ann Cobb, September 15, 1865.

It might have been an attempt to prove that she could be even more useful to the family in the world to come. No matter what Aggy intended, Mary Ann saw it as the unmasking of a dishonest performance in the world that had been. She felt a deep sense of betrayal by a woman she had viewed as a rock upon whom she might build any structure. She now doubted Aggy's honesty and sincerity. "War and freedom have cleared my house of French China," she wrote. "I am compelled to use my finest China every day, and to my horror and disgust I found Aggy sending the China plates to the kitchen. . . . I stopped that and hunted up the odd pieces . . . but when I am absent, the China will begin to circulate among the darkies. Oh Freedom! How many abuses have been committed in thy name—*Legions*."[33] Her moral revulsion at the thought of freedpeople passing around her china was only surpassed by her dismay that Aggy had aligned herself with them rather than herself. By 1867, Mary Ann was bitterly denouncing the behavior of her servants as they attempted to define new boundaries as employees and free people. "I shall cease to look for quality and honesty in the negro race," she fumed. "Give me white servants. . . . There is no more comfort or satisfaction in having negroes around us."[34]

Mary Ann employed Aggy for a few years more, but her doubts surrounding Aggy's loyalty continued to fester. Howell's sudden death in 1868 pushed her to a breaking point. The world she had been born into was gone. Everything she had worked for, all she had invested in her husband's political career, and all she had sacrificed during the war had come to nothing. The gilt on her life had been scoured away. Her son's simultaneous fuming over Isaac's embrace of Radical Republicanism made matters even worse. Howell Jr. threatened to fire Isaac if he exercised his newly acquired suffrage to vote the Republican ticket, warning, "He shall be fully informed before he polls his votes, [as] my house cannot be divided."[35]

Isaac's perceived treachery hardened Mary Ann's fear that Aggy had

33. Mary Ann Cobb to Howell Cobb, June 24, 1867.

34. Mary Ann Cobb to Howell Cobb, October 1, 1867. On the crumbling of the facade of deference, and white responses to it, see Stephanie E. Jones-Rogers, "A Most Unprecedented Robbery," chap. 8 in *They Were Her Property: White Women as Slave Owners in the American South* (New Haven: Yale University Press, 2019); Thavolia Glymph, *Out of the House of Bondage: The Transformation of the Plantation Household* (Cambridge, UK: Cambridge University Press, 2008), 97–166; Clarke, *Dwelling Place*, 449–51; Jane Turner Censer, *The Reconstruction of White Southern Womanhood* (Baton Rouge: Louisiana State University Press, 2003), 60–71.

35. Howell Cobb Jr. to Mary McKinley Cobb, December 27, 1868.

been merely performing a role for all of their decades together. She could not lean upon this woman, whom she once "trust[ed] so entirely," in her hour of grief. Isolated and bitter over all she had lost in blood and faith, she now viewed Aggy as just another wage laborer. Soon after, a desperately ill Aggy wrote Mary Ann requesting unpaid wages and apologizing for the illness that kept her from work. "Please excuse me," she begged, "as I am in need." Despite the tension that had grown between the two women since emancipation, or perhaps to guard against it, she again pledged her loyalty and swore, "I will work for you just as long as you wants me."[36] These professions of fidelity merely stirred Mary Ann's skepticism. Aggy had proven adept at reading the complexities of master-slave relationships but failed to appreciate how loss had affected her former mistress. By the 1870s, she had been pushed out of Mary Ann's affection. Aggy periodically worked for the Cobb children into the 1880s but apparently never worked for Mary Ann again.

Aggy's departure from the Cobb house marked the culmination of a process rather than a beginning. She and Isaac had learned from experience that to enjoy their freedom most fully they needed to escape the domineering presence of their enslavers-turned-employers. Using money saved from their labor and the fifty dollars per year that General Taylor had bequeathed to Isaac in his will, in 1866 they constructed a home on a lot in Athens purchased from Marion Cobb, widow of Howell's younger brother Thomas. Isaac's brother, Edward, purchased the adjoining lot, allowing them to raise their children side-by-side in a tight family network.[37] Both branches of the Mills family lived next to each other for at least the next twenty-five years, and the cousins remained, as one of them later recounted, "near and dear to each other" throughout their lives.[38]

Aggy and Isaac's selection of a homesite proved strategic.[39] It allowed Aggy to walk to work at the Cobb house but also enabled her to raise her children among other freedpeople in what was quickly becoming one of Athens's first African American neighborhoods. As the neighborhood

36. Aggy Mills to Mary Ann Cobb, undated manuscript.

37. Deed of Sale from Isaac Mills to Aggy Mills, May 22, 1866, Clarke County Superior Court, Clarke County, Georgia, Deed Book Y, 113.

38. Nanny Mills to Howell Cobb Jr., July 1901, Cobb Family Papers, Hargrett Rare Book and Manuscript Library, University of Georgia, Athens.

39. Michael L. Thurmond, *A Story Untold: Black Men and Women in Athens History*, 3rd ed. (Athens: Deeds Publishing, 2019), 10–23; Kaye, *Joining Places*, 209–20; Glenda Elizabeth Gilmore, *Gender and Jim Crow: Women and the Politics of White Supremacy in North Carolina, 1896–1920* (Chapel Hill: University of North Carolina Press, 1996), 10–14, 15–18.

grew around them, its residents eagerly sought a school for their children. Aggy, perhaps more than any of them, understood the value of education. She likely had been teaching her daughters long before freedom came. She knew that a formal education would create opportunities for them to move beyond the limits of domestic servitude.

The American Missionary Association established the Knox School in Athens in 1867.[40] Aggy and Isaac were strong supporters of the venture and helped raise funds for the new building. Despite his illiteracy, Isaac became the institution's treasurer.[41] Louisa and Fanny were among the first students. Their mother's literacy had once been illegal, but the girls learned her lessons well. One of their teachers wrote of them, "[Fanny] is one of the best readers in my school. And both have mastered the 4 Fundamental rules of Arith[metic], have been several times through Mitchells First Lessons [of Geography] and are able to give the name of almost any part of speech."[42] They embraced education not only as a personal opportunity but also as an obligation to their community. They understood the promise of the Knox School as a chance to escape from domestic servitude, elevate the role of all freedpeople, and train the next generation of African American voters.[43] Both aspired to become teachers.

Aggy and Isaac supported their daughters' ambitions. In 1843 a teenage Aggy had stood waiting for the auctioneer's hammer to fall and announce her fate. Twenty-six years later she watched her own teenage daughter depart for college. Louisa enrolled at Atlanta University, aiming to become a professional version of the teacher her mother had always been. Unfortunately a financial setback in the family soon left her parents unable to afford the cost, and Louisa returned home. She ac-

---

40. F. E. Morgan to Rev. E. P. Smith, April 17, 1867, field letters of the American Missionary Association, Amistad Research Center, New Orleans (microfilm, University of Georgia Libraries). The American Missionary Association was a philanthropic society, founded in New York in 1846, that established schools for freedpeople across the Reconstruction South.

41. W. C. Lewis to Miss Eliza C. Ayer, December 6, 1869, and C. A. Drake to Revd E. P. Smith, January 17, 1870, field letters of the American Missionary Association.

42. L. J. Kelley to Rev. E. P. Smith, February 1, 1868, field letters of the American Missionary Association.

43. On education of freedpeople, see Gilmore, *Gender and Jim Crow*, 14, 31–38, 45–51. See also Ronald E. Butchart, *Schooling the Freed People: Teaching, Learning, and the Struggle for Black Freedom, 1861–1876* (Chapel Hill: University of North Carolina Press, 2010); Joe M. Richardson, *Christian Reconstruction: The American Missionary Association and Southern Blacks, 1861–1890* (Tuscaloosa: University of Alabama Press, 1986); Jacqueline Jones, *Soldiers of Light and Love: Northern Teachers and Georgia Blacks, 1865–1873* (Athens: University of Georgia Press, 1980); Ronald E. Butchart, *Northern Schools, Southern Blacks, and Reconstruction: Freedmen's Education* (Westport, Conn.: Greenwood Press, 1980).

cepted a teaching position at Knox but continued to dream of completing her education so she could ultimately "go away to some distant land to teach."[44] She never got her wish. Professional frustration continued to plague her. At the end of her first year as a teacher, low student enrollment prompted the school to eliminate her position.

The school's remaining teacher, "Miss Brooks," noted, "[Louisa] feels a little hard because she is not employed this year," but she offered no sympathy or assistance. "She would like to go to Atlanta *one* more term and asked me if I did not think Mr. Cravath would help her go, I replied that I did not know but I did not think he would. I learned when quite small to help myself and I do not know that I have as much sympathy as I ought for one who will come to me with kid gloves and fur tippet on and ask me to let her come for half prices as her mother is poor."[45] Undeterred, Louisa opened her own private school in Athens. Several years later, however, she married Alfred Mills, possibly a distant relation of her father, and by 1880 had left her school to stay at home with her two children and two stepchildren. She returned to the classroom one last time when public schools opened in Athens in 1886, but only taught for one year.[46]

Fanny avoided many of the professional challenges of her sister and enjoyed a long and successful career. She married Robert Lewis sometime around 1882 and gave birth to one son. The records of both her personal and professional life, however, are sparse. It seems likely that her parents supported her in the same ways they supported her sister, but the extent of her postsecondary education remains unclear. She taught in Athens's public schools for decades and eventually became principal of the city's Brooklyn School in 1904. Over thirty-eight years as a teacher and principal she shaped the educations and lives of thousands of African American students.[47]

44. Atlanta University, *Catalogue of the Normal and Preparatory Departments of Atlanta University* (Atlanta: Atlanta University, 1870); Louisa Mills to Rev. E. M. Cravath, June 5, 1871, field letters of the American Missionary Association, Amistad Research Center, New Orleans (microfilm, University of Georgia Libraries).

45. N. D. Brooks to Rev. E. M. Cravath, November 15, 1871, field letters of the American Missionary Association, Amistad Research Center, New Orleans (microfilm, University of Georgia Libraries).

46. W. C. Lewis to Miss Eliza C. Ayer, December 6, 1869; C. A. Drake to Revd E. P. Smith, January 17, 1870, ibid.; U.S. Census, 1880, Clarke County, Georgia; Clarke County Board of Education Papers, vol. 20, Hargrett Rare Book and Manuscript Library, University of Georgia, Athens.

47. U.S. Census, 1900, Clarke County, Georgia; Clarke County Board of Education Papers, vols. 20, 22, and 25.

It is tempting to celebrate Louisa's and Fanny's professional lives as markers of the universe balancing itself, making up for past evils, but the quiet truth of it is that they simply went on to live lives. Ordinary, prosaic, everyday lives. They grew up, married, raised families, and did work that served a need and fulfilled their souls. There may not be karmic realignment in their stories, but there is a certain beauty in recognizing that their parents both lived long enough to see how it all ended. From their small house in Athens, Aggy and Isaac watched their daughters go out into the world, grandchildren arrive, and change come.

Mary Ann Cobb died in 1889 of complications arising from a stroke, thirty-five years into the new world the war had left in its wake. She was nearly blind and partially paralyzed. Although she was surrounded by a large family, and despite living several short blocks away from the Mills house, she breathed her last without the comfort of the woman who had once been her closest companion. There is no record of Aggy or Isaac recognizing her death.

Isaac Mills died the following year at age sixty-three. After his death, Aggy briefly returned to the service of the Cobb family. Although the bonds of affection between Mary Ann and Aggy had disintegrated after the war, the Cobb children never abandoned their close relationship with the woman who had raised them. When Howell and Mary Ann's niece Marion "Birdie" Cobb needed a nursemaid to care for her children, Aggy answered the call. Birdie's husband, Hoke Smith, was appointed secretary of the interior in the cabinet of President Grover Cleveland in 1893. Aggy was a natural choice to help the young family navigate the nation's capital, as she had previously played the same role there for Howell and Mary Ann in the 1840s and 1850s.[48]

Aggy lived to see the dawn of the twentieth century but died in Athens soon after, following a protracted illness.[49] Given that her birth was unannounced and uncelebrated, her life valued as an object to be auctioned and sold, and her true freedom so hard won, it might have surprised her to find that all of Athens stopped to take notice of her passing. The Athens *Daily Banner* solemnly mourned the death of a woman "well-known to both white and colored," who had been "loved and esteemed by both relatives and friends."[50] More importantly, the Cobb children stopped to

48. *Athens Banner*, April 26, 1912.

49. "Obituary," undated newspaper clipping, Mary McKinley Cobb Papers, Hargrett Rare Book and Manuscript Library, University of Georgia, Athens.

50. Ibid.

take notice of her passing too. One of them carefully trimmed Aggy's obituary from the local newspaper and preserved it alongside the obituaries of immediate family members. She was the only formerly enslaved person they honored this way.

The ties between the Mills and Cobb families persisted, even after Aggy's death. As her niece Nanny Mills reminded Howell Cobb Jr. of the roots of their bonds in a letter dated the following year, "Fannie Cousin Lou an all know . . . you thought so much of there Dear mama for no one on Earth could not have shown a better heart or been better to anyone than you was to Aggie."[51] Accounts from both families' descendants indicate that their lives remained interwoven until at least the mid-twentieth century. Even generations later, they recalled, their families continued to interact, seek each other's advice, and affectionately call each other "cousin."[52]

The enslaved Aggy was first recorded in the world as a young girl, a piece of property forced to stand on the steps of a grand house and await fate meted out by an auctioneer's hammer. That experience shaped all the decades of her life. It taught her that she alone must shoulder the burden of protecting those she cared about most. Their safety required her to employ the few tools she possessed to convince Mary Ann, through countless daily interactions, that she and her family were loyal, dedicated, and completely irreplaceable. Her success at meeting this challenge carried first her father and brother and then Isaac, Louisa, and Fanny over the rocky shoals of slavery and eventually into the safe harbor of emancipation. Half a century after the auctioneer's hammer fell, a few blocks from where it began, Aggy Carter Mills died in a house all her own, a wife, a grandmother, and a free woman.

———————————

51. Nanny Mills to Howell Cobb Jr., July 1901.

52. Agnes Amos, telephone conversations with the authors, July 8, October 5, and October 16, 2013. Mrs. Amos, who grew up in the house Aggy and Isaac built, was the last family descendant to vividly remember Fanny and Louisa. Mrs. Amos's account is corroborated by multiple conversations between 2013 and 2020 with Milton Leathers, the great-great-grandson of Howell and Mary Ann Cobb.

Sarah Rootes Cobb to Mary Ann Cobb

Cowpens Plantation, [1842–1843]

Our minds were greatly relieve by your letter by Bob. We had endured intense anxiety about the sale . . . and poor Aggy for whom I have suffered much. I felt for all the negroes, but for her, I did keenly feel as I never could reconcile it to myself for her or her brothers or sisters to be sold if it could by any lawful means be prevented. The others I hope my dear Howell will be able to get back at some future day, if the Lord see's fit to order it so. If not we ought to be contented and bow in submission to his divine will.

Bill of Sale for Aggy Carter

Clarke County, October 21, 1843

Whereas, by virtue of a writ of Fieri Facias, to me directed, from the Honorable Superior Court of said County whereas the Bank of the State of Georgia [damaged] Cobb Indorser[53] was defendant [damaged] levy on a certain negro girl named Aggy about Seventeen Years of age.

Which said negro girl being by me advertised according to law, was, on the fourth day of October, Instant, exposed to public sale and outcry, at the house of Howell Cobb in the town of Athens in satisfaction of the said Execution, when John B. Lamar being the highest bidder, the said Negro Girl was knocked off to him for the sum of four hundred Dollars.

Now therefore, I, James Hendon, Sheriff of the County aforesaid, for and in consideration of the sum of four hundred Dollars, to me in hand paid by the [damaged] ledged, have bargained, sold and delivered, and by these presents do bargain [damaged] the said John B. Lamar the said Negro [damaged] which said Negro girl I do warrant and defend unto the said John B. Lamar his heirs and assigns forever, as far as by law a Sheriff is bound [damaged] warrant and defend in such case.

In witness whereof, I have hereunto set my hand to seal, this twenty first day of October, 1843.

---

53. Howell Cobb is identified here by the legal term "Indorser," as his financial troubles resulted from cosigning his father's loans.

Mary Ann Cobb to Howell Cobb

Cowpens Plantation, December 10, 1843

Lamar asked me very gamely to let him read Papa's letter, he unfolded it
and looked over it a while, folded it up and, handed it back to me, after-
wards he told Aggy that he had read his Papa's letter, says she what did
you read Bajor,[54] "I read A and B."

Sarah Rootes Cobb to Mary Ann Cobb

Cowpens Plantation, February 18, 1844

Your dear little boys keep quite well and are as lively as birds . . . . I keep
Aggy with them constantly, and she appears very careful of them.

Sarah Rootes Cobb to Mary Ann Cobb

Cowpens Plantation, March 10, 1844

Tonight they went to sleep talking to Aggy about catching fish tomorrow
in the spring. She is a first rate nurse and I expect you will find it hard for
Bajor to give her up when you return.

Sarah Rootes Cobb to Mary Ann Cobb

Cowpens Plantation, May 1, 1844

I carried [the boys] over to Sister Milly's this evening, and they both
wanted to stay, and Sissa wanted to come home with me, I told them they
might stay if they chose to leave their poor Grandma without a single
child, and Aggy should take Sissa and we would go home, they both then
bawled for Aggy and came home without any more trouble.

---

54. The family nickname for Lamar Cobb, Howell and Mary Ann's third son.

Sarah Rootes Cobb to Mary Ann Cobb

Cowpens Plantation, December 8, 1844

Aggy has got a red bird for [the boys] in thier cage and it affords them a good deal of amusement, she is very attentive to them and they are all very fond of her.

Sarah Rootes Cobb to Mary Ann Cobb

Cowpens Plantation, January 1, 1845

[Howell] threw Johnny's sock in the fire and it was burnt past mending before Aggy could get it out, Johnny could not well spare it, I have set on one for Aggy to knit and she has promised to be very smart at it. . . . Aggy has suffered a good deal with toothache and a bad cold, but not bad enough for her to neglect the children.

Sarah Rootes Cobb to Mary Ann Cobb

Cowpens Plantation, January 5, 1845

Rachal & Aggy are well and with the other servants send thier respects to you and love to Sylvia remember us all to her.

Sarah Rootes Cobb to Mary Ann Cobb

Cowpens Plantation, January 8, 1845

John A came tonight to say his letters to me, so I might write you word how he was progressing. He knows all the large ones very well except three, Aggy I expect will be very zealous in her teaching of them, she says Bajer knows as far as D.

Sarah Rootes Cobb to Mary Ann Cobb

Cowpens Plantation, January 22, 1845

Bajer brought his book to Laura this evening to say his lesson, I believe Aggy is trying hard to teach them, she has finished one pr of socks for John A and commenced another. . . . Rachel keeps very well and with Aggy and the other servants send thier respects to you and love to Sylvia.

John B. Lamar to Mary Ann Cobb

Macon, May 11, 1845

When you get settled again, if you need a boy about the yard, Robert, Aggys brother perhaps might suit you. He is in every respect like George, amiable, tractable, not very smart, but as much so as George.

Sarah Rootes Cobb to Mary Ann Cobb

Cowpens Plantation, November 23, 1845

Someone asked Bajer who he loved the most, he said Papa Mama and Aggy, oh says I do you love Aggy better than Grandma, the dear little fellow answered no directly.

Sarah Rootes Cobb to Mary Ann Cobb

Cowpens Plantation, December 1, 1845

I suppose Aggy is enjoying herself finely, she has hardly had time yet to see all the sights.[55]

---

55. Mary Ann returned briefly to the Cowpens in November 1845. When she returned to Washington, D.C., at the end of the month, she took Aggy with her as a nursemaid and left Sylvia in Georgia. According to Agnes Amos, Aggy later told her children that she concealed Mary Ann's jewelry inside her dress whenever they traveled to and from the federal capital. Agnes Amos, telephone conversations with the authors, July 8, October 5, and October 16, 2013.

Sarah Rootes Cobb [writing as John A. Cobb II] to Mary Ann Cobb

Cowpens Plantation, December 18, 1845

Tell [Howell Jr. and Henry] they must kiss Aggy for brother and me, we want to see her too. . . . Mammy Sylvia Aunt Rachell & all the servants send thier best respects to Papa & you and love to Aggy.

Sarah Rootes Cobb [writing as John A. Cobb II] to Mary Ann Cobb

Cowpens Plantation, January 15, [1846][56]

Tell Aggy I expect she has seen and heard so much she will have a plenty of fine story's to tell us for years to come. All us boys send our love to her and so does all the servants.

Louisa Dobbin[57] to Mary Ann Cobb

Washington, D.C., June 17, 1846

Tilla sends her love to Aggy.

E. A. McKay[58] to Mary Ann Cobb

Mt. Pleasant, N.C., July 22, 1846

Caty sends howdy to you & children & to Aggy asks Aggy if she is married, tell Silvey howdy for me.

---

56. Sarah misdated this letter 1845. Mary Ann's reply to it and the preceding letter makes clear that both documents date to January 1846.

57. Wife of James Dobbin, U.S. congressman from North Carolina.

58. Wife of James McKay, U.S. congressman from North Carolina.

Sarah Rootes Cobb to Howell Cobb

Cowpens Plantation, September 18, 1847

Little Basil begins to stand alone and tries hard to talk. Aggy is very attentive to him & indeed to them all and it is very seldom you hear a cry, indeed I have not heard Basil cry but very little when she would be washing
him, since you left.

Sarah Rootes Cobb to Howell Cobb

Cowpens Plantation, October 21, 1847

Dear little Basil has heard his Grandpa talk so much about the [mosqui-
toes] and seeing Aggy kill them, that he will blow at them & slap his hand
against the wall to kill them. It would amuse you to see him.

Mary Ann Cobb to Howell Cobb

Athens, January 15, 1849

I have a great hurdle ahead of me this next month. . . . I shall be put up
to all my ingenuity continuing to do without [Rachel], as she is my chief
house servant. And now it takes Aggy till ten o'clock to get mine and the
childrens rooms cleaned after dressing the four boys. I dress the baby, rising at daylight.

Mary Ann Cobb to Howell Cobb

Athens, November 24, 1849

Howell came home full of Miss Lees, or Lee as he pleases to call her, saying that she was his sweetheart, and Lee had promised to wait for him.
But says Aggy you are too young, "Never mind," says H. "She said she
would wait for me, and you know I will soon be grown."

Mary Ann Cobb to Howell Cobb

Athens, December 25, 1849

Shortly after a band of negro musicians, beaux of Aggy's came into the yard, serenading. The boys were up in a moment and Lamar soon dressed, and would have gone out immediately, but I objected. It had been agreed upon previously between Coleman and my boys, that they were to come out when the music struck up. They performed two times for the benefit of the white family, before the back piazza and then adjourned to Rachel's house, where they found the colored ladies sitting up. . . .

So far the Christmas has been dull to white people.

Sarah Rootes Cobb to Howell Cobb

Athens, February 25, 1850

Aggy alarmed us all very much yesterday morning, she had something of a fit, Dr. Moore said she had Cholic, we sent for him at once, she is much better today and I hope will soon be about again.

Sarah Rootes Cobb to Howell Cobb

Athens, March 6, 1850

Mary Ann also wishes me to say to you, that she is much worried in her mind about who she shall take on to nurse for her. If Aggy gets well enough to nurse she can do nothing else but attend to the baby, and she does not know if you have made any arrangements about the cleaning up of the bedrooms, as there will be more to clean up than you use now. . . . I do hope Aggy will get well enough to go with her, as I think her the best nurse I ever saw, she has kept up ever since I wrote you she was better, and Dr Moore thinks it was a turn in her disease and she would now get well.

Mary Ann Cobb to Howell Cobb
Athens, March 26, 1850

As Aggy's health is indifferent, I will have to supply her place with some one who can sleep in my room particularly in the event of her marrying, which she will probably do when Maj Taylor allows his servant to marry.

Mary Ann Cobb to Howell Cobb
Athens, September 2, 1850

The principal reason for my writing today is to get your permission for Aggy to enter into the bonds of wedlock. Genl Taylor's body-servant Isaac Mills, a good looking mulato boy of good character as far as I can learn, is the applicant for her fair hand. He has gotten his Masters consent, which the parties esteemed the greatest obstacle [to] overcome. He gave me a call last evening and told me his wish. I answered that I had no objections as I was willing for Aggy to consult her own wishes, but that I would have to consult you before I gave a final answer. You will be pleased to return an answer by the next mail, as you can well remember your experience in waiting for an answer, and will doubtless have too much sympathy for a *fellow lover* than to make the happy swain wait "*three weeks.*" He presumed that I could get an answer from you in a *week*, he will be looking anxiously with a palpitating heart for the close of this week, therefore be kind & considerate. The willing couple, contemplate marrying on the 20th of this month, presuming your answer is favorable.

Howell Cobb to Mary Ann Cobb
Washington, D.C., September 6, 1850

In reply to the application of Aggys lover I cheerfully give my assent, as yours has been obtained.

Mary Ann Cobb to Howell Cobb

Athens, September 14, 1850

I have commenced preparations for Aggy's & Isaacs wedding, not Isaac of old, whom Mr Harris discourses to have been 70 years old when he was married—for he is only 23 according to Miss Burne's recollection—Mary is head baker and Cousin Cornelia, Sarah, Mattie & Josephine Segan are all helping her, with lively interest. I walk around as superintendent, and my noddel[59] is as confused as an addled egg.

Mary Ann Cobb to Howell Cobb

Athens, September 20, 1850

A day or two since I went out shopping with Cousin Cornelia, Milly and Mattie, and separating, Mattie and I went to the milliners to purchase some bridal ornaments for Aggy while Milly & Cousin Cornelia went to the book store. . . .

Tomorrow is the wedding day the 21st the Equinox, unfortunately. Last night we had a heavy rain, but as it is now clear I hope the darkies will have a clear night. The girls helped me throughout with the cake and Mary is coming today to help dress it, and in return I shall invite some 8 or 10 beaux for them to spend their time agreeably. Miss Burnes & the younger Taylors have expressed a desire to witness the marriage and of course they are to be here, Miss Callie also, Tom & Marion, Milly, Eddy and Jimmy Lumpkin, making altogether a family party. . . .

There have been about 196 tickets issued. Cousin Cornelia & I have occupied the whole of yesterday writing the tickets. I shall send to Capt Dorsey to be here, to keep order.

Sep 21st—I wrote in haste yesterday and today I am all in confusion, cleaning up the kitchen making salad, cutting loaf bread, washing plates & dishes etc and I would not send this letter but to relieve your mind from apprehensions. . . . Aggy is [in] a fine spirit, and takes every minute that the baby sleeps to fix her room and apparel.

---

59. A Middle English word for head.

Mary Ann Cobb to Howell Cobb

Athens, September 25, 1850

Aggy's wedding and the girls party went off gloriously. I never saw negroes and white people enjoy themselves more.

Mary Ann Cobb to Howell Cobb

Athens, December 17, 1850

This morning Aggy is in bed with what she thinks is *cold*, but I rather suspect it is the natural *result* of *marriage*.

Varina Davis[60] to Mary Ann Cobb

Brierfield, Mississippi, January 13, 1851

Now if you would come over to Mississippi, and bring Mattie, and Sarah, and Hessie, and Mary, and Howell, and Bajor, and Johnny, and dear little Maran, and last, still not least dear little Aggy, I would make my house look cheerful for you, and then we could have grand times.

Mary Ann Cobb to Howell Cobb

Athens, July 23, 1851

On the 18th about [11:00 a.m.] Aggy gave birth to a daughter. Her baby is small but healthy, and Aggy has been as well as anyone could.

---

60. Wife of U.S. senator Jefferson Davis, future secretary of war under President Pierce. In 1861, Howell Cobb, as president of the Provisional Confederate Congress, administered the oath of office to inaugurate Davis as president of the Confederate States of America.

Mary Ann Cobb to Howell Cobb
Athens, August 27, 1851

Aggy is still suffering with her breast. Dr Moore says it will not break before Sunday. Of course she is no use to me tho' her babe is scarcely 6 weeks old.

Mary Ann Cobb to Howell Cobb
Athens, September 2, 1851

Aggy is still of no help to me tho' her babe is in its seventh week. I am therefore annoyed a good deal with housekeeping.

Mary Ann Cobb to Howell Cobb
Athens, September 21, 1851

Aggy is still disabled by her breast. It has finally risen and broken naturally, by the constant application of plaster and poultices, recommended by Old Eady, and she is much relieved. I do trust this will be the last of her suffering for it has been very great.

John B. Lamar to Mary Ann Cobb
Macon, October 15, 1851

I would carry Rachel, Aggy Eliza & Burton to Milledgeville. . . . As to Eliza I think you would find use for her too. Aunt Sylvia can take care of the lot.[61]

---

61. John B. was advising his sister on preparations for moving to the Governor's Mansion in Milledgeville following Howell's election as governor of Georgia.

Robert Taylor to Howell Cobb

Athens, May 21, 1852

My man Isaac who has a wife in your yard, and belonging to you, applied
to me last evening for the privilege of visiting her. I replied that I was going down to [Milledgeville] in a week, and that he could accompany me.
He replied that she would be gone in that time, and seemed much dis-
turbed. I thought no more of it until I learned that he was missing this
morning. He has no doubt gone down to see his wife, he may have been
informed that she was about leaving for a distance, and as he is very fond
of his wife, may have been induced to take this unfortunate step in consequence. . . . I would take it as exceedingly kind if you may see him to have
him well secured in jail . . . he left me without any cause.

Mary Ann Cobb to Sarah Martha "Mattie" Cobb

Athens, July 28, [1852]

Today Aggy Howell & I were discoursing upon the subject of your staying in New York so long. Aggy remarked that she thought you were right
as you might never get another chance unless you were all married. "But
says Howell suppose they never marry." "Then they cant go replied Aggy."
"Then they will be old batchelors says Howell. Oh! no, says A. they cant
be so! Well then they will be *Mrs* batchelors says H." Aggy then gave him
the Misses Polks as happy examples. I think Howell has softened the term
of Old Maid considerably. Mrs. Batchelor is not certainly as offensive as
"Old Maid."

Mary Ann Cobb to Laura Rutherford

Roswell, August 11, 1852

I am grateful to you for your kind offer respecting my children. I hope
you will not be hurt at my declining it. It is important *to me* to have Aggy
attend Mary Ann[62] night and day, as there is no other servant, I can trust

---

62. Mary Ann Lamar Cobb, the eldest daughter of Howell and Mary Ann.

so entirely with my children, and in consequence of Aggy's having an infant, she could not accompany Mary Ann to your house.

Mary Ann Cobb to Howell Cobb Jr.

Milledgeville, February 20, 1854

Tell Aggy I shall expect her to do wonders this year in the way of eggs and chickens. . . . Your sister is getting smarter and more interesting every day. . . . She sits up until 9 o'clock, to favor Polly's enjoying a little of kitchen society after tea, and she will not stir a step towards bed until I move. It will require a good deal of Aggy's oily talk to induce her to go back with a good grace to her "sunset tea and biscuit."

Mary Ann Cobb to Howell Cobb Jr.

Athens, December 16, 1854

[Mary Ann] sits quietly every morning whilst Aggy dresses her, and tells her stories of the "Babes in the wood," "Leap over my Thumb," "Beauty and the Beast," etc.

Mary Ann Cobb to Howell Cobb

Athens, June 27, 1855

Mary Ann . . . said very dolefully I wish *you* would let Eliza nurse *the baby*, and let Aggy *nurse me*. Sylvia is cooking, and Aggy nursing.

Mary Ann Cobb to John B. Lamar

Athens, June 29, 1855

Mary Ann has drawn out her hammock again . . . She and Lou and Jenny[63] were swinging each other in it joyously. . . . I had it not in my heart to check her amusement, she goes so heart, soul and body into ev-

---

63. Aggy's and Rachel's daughters, respectively.

erything she undertakes. This morning, Aggy had Sarah lying in it, and you would have been delighted to have seen the complacent look of comfort and enjoyment which beamed from those old looking eyes, as she swung from side to side in the hammock.

Sarah Rootes Cobb to Mary Ann Cobb
West Point, January 18, 1856

[With] Eliza not being well you will be more worried with only Bena, if I was you I should send for Aggy & let her leave her child with its Grandmother.[64]

Howell Cobb to Mary Ann Cobb
Washington, D.C., February 24, 1856

I told Aggy, that you wanted her to go to Washington & she says she is willing to go with you & I have no doubt will go cheerfully.

Mary Ann Cobb to John A. Cobb II
Macon, March 1, 1856

I send you a list of clothes which I wish Aggy to get and make up for herself, by the 1st of April. Give the paper to her and tell her to take it immediately to Cobb & Crawford,[65] and get good articles. I will put in also Louisa's summer clothes as Aggy will like to make them before she goes. Tell Aggy to turn over to Rachel *my sewing* which she has not finished, and go *about her own sewing at once.* Tell Aggy to give Rachel the directions about the work just as I wrote them, and say to Rachel, I shall look for the work to be finished, when I come, and done neatly.

---

64. Isaac's mother, Dorcas, who was in the Taylor household.
65. A general store in downtown Athens owned in part by John B. Cobb.

Mary Ann Cobb to Howell Cobb

Athens, March 31, 1856

Dorcas, Aggy's mother-in-law is in *very low* health, and I am unwilling to leave Louisa with her 'till she is well enough to take care of her. Isaac will be up the country[66] till the 1st of May, and if I leave the 15th of April, that will be only two weeks that Lou will be with her grandmother before her father comes.

Sarah Rootes Cobb to Mary Ann Cobb

Athens, April 17, 1856

Rachel came out to bring me the things you left for me and for which I return you my sincere thanks. I asked her how Dorcas was, she said she was still very bad off, all were well on your lot & so was Aggy's little girl.

Mary Ann Cobb to Howell Cobb Jr.

Washington, D.C., April 30, 1856

[Your father] sent "Taylor" our man servant in search of the monkey man, authorized to offer him a dollar to come. . . . The crowd were in ecstasies with the performance, and baby Sarah was then looking on with her sharp eyes, and now when Aggy tells her to dance like the monkey, she will stick out one foot and go thro' the motions. . . .

Aggy rides her out near to the President's or the Capitol frequently, and the "fat baby" is a spectacle of itself. Many ladies stop to enquire whose child it is, and those who know your father of course see a striking resemblance to him.

---

66. Isaac accompanied Taylor on his yearly tour of his plantations.

Howell Cobb Jr. to Mary Ann Cobb

Athens, May 31, 1856

Tell Aggy that I saw Isaac and Lou both the other day and they were very well.

Mary Ann Cobb to Howell Cobb Jr.

Washington, D.C., June 7, 1856

When you write again tell me about Lamar Louisa & Isaac my gardens grass & Roses. Aggy is well and desires to be remembered to you and send her love to Isaac & Lou.

Mary Ann Cobb to Howell Cobb

Athens, September 14, 1856

Mary Ann . . . went off cheerfully to school, Sarah and Aggy accompanying her. Aggy goes for her at twelve and holds an umbrella over her on returning, and in the afternoon Sarah goes down in her little carriage drawn by Aggy, to bring her home.

Aggy Mills to "My dar little misstrs"

Athens, March [1857]

My dar littel misstrs

 I hav ben wanting to rite to you for sum time but I could not rite as I had one of my eyes badly hurt. Thar for I hope you will not think that I am ungratful to you and my daer missters for the nice and handsum persants that she sent to me and my childran. Oh I do wish that it was in my power to rite how gratful and thankful I am to you and I hope the lord well spar me long ornuf to rase my childran to feel the same. Lu [joins] me in menny thanks to you and frances wod too if she new her duty. I am truly glad to hare that you all will be home this spring. Oh how happy I will be to see your daer littel [damaged] agan and more then happy to see the littel [damaged] that is srangger to me. I want to see her dar littel [face] very much inded.

The trees and flowers ar puting out very pretty hear & now but we hav a grat del of rane. Miss Milly Cobb has got very well agane. Miss hasy has a fine sun and miss adda has a fine dorter all douing very well. That is all of the nuse that I no of. All [damaged] well [illegible] Reuthafords [damaged] Lamar coms up to see the flowers [damaged]. Thar has been sum of the prettyest hyersuns hear that I ever saw and tha was very much admirard by the ladys.

I hope you well excuse my spellig as thar is grat meny mestaks.

your humble sirvent
Agnes Mills

Ples gave my love to ant silve and girls

Mary Ann Cobb to Howell Cobb

Athens, March 31, 1857

Aggy's child was very bad off last night, but better today. Aggy has been sitting up with it for three nights, until last night one of her friends in the neighborhood came and sat up and let her sleep. Aggy I fear is taking the epidemic cold.

Mary Ann Cobb to Howell Cobb

Athens, June 27, 1857

Aggy is doing well, so is her babe.[67] She will be on her feet long before I leave.

---

67. Mary Ann references the birth of Aggy and Isaac's second daughter, Fanny.

Mary Ann Cobb to Howell Cobb

Athens, July 10, 1857

Sarah rejoices in the possession of a "hoop" (skirt). Ever since her sister
had one, she has been pleading for a hoop "Me want a hoop." I cut out
one for her and Aggy made it, and her delight was great. While it was un-
derway, she would ask all she saw, "Did you know Mudder (Aggy) is making me a hoop."

Mary Ann Cobb to "My Dear Son"

Washington, D.C., September 24, 1857

[Mary Ann] asked Sarah which she wanted to see most Aggy or Lou. She
said Aggy, but *the baby* most of all, "because Aggy let me hold it."

Aggy Mills to Howell Cobb Jr.

Athens, November 2, [1857]

My daer Mas howell

I reseved your wellcom letter of the 20 and I am not Able to tel how
happy I was to think that my young Master thort of me whar thar is so
meny mor importon thengs [illegible] to think of then I am. You want
to know how all of your pets are geting on sence you left hear. Tha are
all well and doing well. Dount gave you self eny unesness abute suggs
nor eny thing that you hav left in my car for you know I am all was glad
to du enny thing to ples you. Thar for I well never negect them for enny
thing. Suggs is just as fat as he can be tho not as tame as he was when you
was har. Your game rooster is looking purttally inded and all of the orther thickens ar well. You want to know [how] the littel darkis ar geting
on. Tha are all [well] except colds. You ask how my littel babey coms on.
I wish sum of the peple thar could see her. I know tha wod think we must
eate sum meet as well as cortton seed[68] oute her[e] for she is the faatest

---

68. The idea of eating cotton seed was a private joke in the household. The Cobbs'
daughter Mary Ann later recalled that it originated when a hired butler in Washington,

colord baby I ever saw. I hav seen white baby much finer tho. Well I belev I hav told you abute all of the thengs that you want to hear. Your littel with hen has not lad an egg sence you left hear. That is all I can think of. I wish I could hear somthing abute miss mary An and miss sharah master Andro. Ples tel them all howdy for me and tel them that I want to see them very much inded. Ples gave my best love to my misstres and tel her that my young masters ar both well.

Ples give my love to mama and polly and elisar. Tel thim that I write to them in a few days. I hav a grad del to tel them when I rite.

> your homble sirvent Aggy

Mary Ann Cobb to John A. Cobb II
Washington, D.C., December 6, 1857

With regard to Serena, I am not committed to Mrs. Baynon[69] . . . and I will leave it entirely with Serena, to say whether she had rather stay with Mrs. Baynon or go to the plantation to her mother. Tell Aggy to talk *privately* with Serena and find out if she wants to stay, and if not send her to the plantation.

Sarah Rootes Cobb to Mary Ann Cobb
Athens, February 11, 1858

Aggy came to see me on sunday. I dont know when I ever saw her look as well. She has fattened up a great deal. She said all were well on the lot.

D.C., asked Aggy, "Mrs. Mills, is it true that down South they feed you on cotton seed?" She retorted, "Do I look like I was fed on cotton seed? . . . Do they feed you up here on oyster shells? Well, they feed us on cotton seed just about as much as they feed you on oyster shells." *Athens Banner*, April 26, 1912.

69. Jane Baynon, wife of Athens merchant Watkins Baynon, who was interested in hiring Serena.

Mary Ann Cobb to John A. Cobb II

Washington, D.C., February 22, 1858

Where is Serena? What does she hire for? I think Aggy mentions her in her letter to Sylvia. I read Aggy's letter easily. Tell her I asked Mary Ann some time since, "If she wanted to write to Aggy." She answered very quickly, "Aggy has'nt written to me." She thought Aggy's letter to Howell was gratuitous.

Mary Ann Cobb to "My Dear Sons"

Washington, D.C., March 29, 1858

I have spent the fore part of the morning in investigating the grievances of the kitchen department, which have from time to time been of a threatening character. Old Mary the cook . . . informed me that Nicholas' brother[70] came every night to our kitchen to give Eliza & Polly lessons in *writing*. I told the old woman I would investigate the charges. . . . I learned from Nicholas that his brother did set copies for my servants, that was all he knew about it, and he did not know it was wrong. I then named it to Sylvia & Polly, and they were silent about the writing, saying that she had told the man she would like him to teach the girls to read, that they might teach her as she had always wanted to learn. . . . "She did not know there was any law in our State against teaching a negro to read." I warned Nicholas that if ever his brother was seen upon our lot, he N would lose his place, and after telling my own of the penalty in our state to a white person found teaching a negro I dismissed them to their respective duties. . . . I am amused with what is going on here.

---

70. A hired butler.

Mary Ann Lamar[71] to Mary Ann Cobb
Athens, August 12, 1858

I went over to your house this morning and saw Aggy and the children. . . . Aggy's baby is not near so pretty as Lu, but it is a strong, large, healthy child, and is very smart. Its Mother says it is ugly.

Mary Ann Cobb to John A. Cobb II
Washington, D.C., August 20, 1858

Attend to this = I want none but our own negroes on the lot, when Isaac is not in Athens. Aggy must look to the *dogs* for protection with Lucius' help. Charge Aggy to take care of Lucius and keep him employed about the lot. Let her take the room Alfred occupied adjoining hers, and let Lucius have a bed in that. This will give her two rooms, she can then cook and eat in the little room = which was the old dining room. Lucius' bed will not be in the way, and she will know at night that he is in his proper place. She must not suffer him to go off the lot at night unless in her company.

Mary Ann Cobb to Howell Cobb Jr.
Athens, May 13, 1859

Mrs. Richard S. Taylor's little daughter came yesterday and asked my daughters to a party at her house today at 4 o'clock. They are upstairs dressing & from the amount of trampling overhead & clatter of heels, I think they are doing their finest. *Aggy* is dressing them, and will go with them, & see that they behave, and eat *proper* things. Do you remember how Aggy used to attend you & guard you at parties?

---

71. Mary Ann's niece, the daughter of Andrew Lamar.

Mary Ann Cobb to Howell Cobb Jr.
Athens, June 16, 1859

Your [pet raccoon] is in fine keeping but is the terror of every other living thing upon the lot. Fanny was coming to the house one morning, and Coonie's chain had gotten out its kinks so that he could come from under the house, and Fanny getting too near him pounced upon her foot, and stuck his claws and teeth in the instep, hurting her so badly, she yelled, and with that the whole lot rose up to rescue her, and if he had not been Mass Howell's coon, I think Aggy would have given him a good drubbing. He is a nuisance. Fanny's foot was badly swelled and had to be poulticed several days and nights to take out the fever and swelling. He ate up a kitten which Aggy gave to Sarah.

Mary Ann Cobb to Howell Cobb
Athens, May 12, 1861

Aggy had the house in nice order. Brother John said everything was so natural and looked so comfortable that it seemed as if I had only made a flying trip of a few days to Augusta or the Springs[72] and returned. Aggy has taste, and she had flowers in vases about the rooms, & everything looked cheerful. She has a fine garden. Peas in abundance.

Mary Ann Cobb to Howell Cobb Jr.
Athens, August 18, 1861

Lizzie[73] was found down at Aggy's house. Aggy was sick & shut up in her house. Aggy asked her who brought [her] she replied "come meself." What for said Aggy. "To see Marmer." She calls Aggy by that name. Said Aggy, how did you get down the steps. "Got down meself."

---

72. Probably Madison Springs, an antebellum resort located several miles northeast of Athens.

73. Howell and Mary Ann's youngest daughter, born October 5, 1859.

Mary Ann Cobb to Howell Cobb

Athens, October 27, 1861

I have a pair of shoes ready to send for *Laurence*,[74] therefore do not buy a pair for him, if he has shoes which will last until John goes on. Aggy's husband makes good strong shoes for two or three dollars, such as perhaps you will have to pay 5 or 6$ for in Va.

Mary Ann Cobb to John B. Lamar

Athens, December 6, 1861

With regard to bringing my "corps of washerwomen," I will bring Melinda. I had been at a loss to know what to do with her until your letter came, giving me permission to bring her. It is a desperate business leaving so many feeble hands with hungry mouths to feed during my absence. I shall leave Ben & Vicey to keep my yards and gardens in order and Aggy will take in sewing to buy wood, etc.

Mary Ann Cobb to John A. Cobb II

Athens, December 29, 1861

We have had rather a dull Christmas. I did not feel in a humor "to make merry" while all the men of our establishment were away from home on a dangerous mission. Funds were too low to invest any in toys, even if I had deemed the occasion fit for such an outlay, and I told the children that Santa Claus had assumed a *neutral* position in imitation of the great European powers....

Aggy made a blue pincushion upon a glass stand for Sarah[75] on her birthday on the 24th. Before Christmas, Fanny said "you children need'nt be hanging up yr stockings, the Yankees have shot down Santa Claus"....

---

74. Rachel's son Lawrence was a body servant to the Cobb sons John Addison II, Lamar, and Howell Jr., who were in the Confederate army serving on their father's staff.

75. Sarah Mildred Cobb, the third daughter of Howell and Mary Ann.

With Aggy's aid I went to work [and] emptied that useful institution "the Mending basket" of its contents, overhauled summer clothing, and made up quite a pile. Aggy was very industrious tumbling the clothes out of the said basket, her department, and I soon heard the solution of her eager charity, when she said, "It does me good to see this basket getting empty."[76] To console her for seeing good calico dresses of the children going away which might have gone next summer to her children, I gave her for Fanny one of Sarah's old silk dresses knowing the antipathy that negroes have to giving things to "poor white people." I told her so, but she asserted she always loved to see me help "poor folks." She already had the little silk dress in hand.

Aggy Mills to Mary Ann Cobb

Athens, January 13, [1862]

My dare misstress

I receivd your moste wellcom letter today and I was veary glad to hear that you had arived safely to macon. I red you letter over and over gane and will do so untel I got it by hart and I intend to cary oute all of your odorous just as if you was hear yourself. My dare misstress I do feal very gratfull to you inded for all of your kindness to me and I feel that it is duty to do all that I can for you at enny time that you call apon me. We are gating along very well with our work. Unkel ben has planted the potatos and the raspberrys. Unkel Ben and myself sends you menny thanks for the money that you sent us. Mr Lamr pade Isac teenty one dollers for you. With he is very thankful to you for. Isac let Gilbut have one doller and sixty cents. Ples remember [me] kindly to all of the littel ladys and the tow littel jenttelmen. I miss them very much but I hope tha ma hav a nice time in macon. Unkel Ben and ant vicy send thar love to the girls and liasar and Anderson.

> your humble sirvant
> Aggy Mills

---

76. Aggy was repairing the Cobb children's old clothes for Mary Ann to donate to soldiers' families.

Aggy Mills to Mary Ann Cobb

Athens, March 11, [1862]

My daer misstres

I rite a few lins to let you know what we aer doing in the garden. We have a bed of peas up and cabbege and collords plants. The potators are coming up very fine. The strawbary vins looks finely. Unkel Ben is very bisay preparing the ground for planting. He wants to know if you wants the Barly path by the stable to stand for seed or must he plant it in corn. He ses the ray [rye] that is the bed in the low garden will not bring much seed. It is tow thin but that on the tares [terrace] by docter longs is growing bautaful. He all so wants to know if you wants the bed to stand in the low garden or not. I have mold up all the taler [tallow] that you left hear. I borld it as white as I could gat it and made one hundred and forty nine candels. I hav just finish to day. I want to make you sum more starch just as sune as the wather gats warm if you have no orther youse for the whete brad and shorts that is hare. It is quite cold hear today. I hav one hen with aght tickens and wod of had fore but the dogs brak them up. I will hav tow more next weake. Isaac ses he hope you will not think hard of him a bute you work. His master has bin quite sake sence he was in macon and it was not in his power to work much but have sum of it dun. His master is going to move to his morgen plantation to live and he has to go but he will do you work thar. He ses if you want enny work dun for the childran pleas to send him word and he will try to doo it befor he levs this place.

All are well heare but Lu she has sor thorth and headack.

The warther is turning quit cold.

your houmble sirvent Aggy

Aggy Mills to Mary Ann Cobb

Athens, March 13, [1862]

My daer mistress

I hav ben wanting to rite to you for sume time but tha hav ben so much passing from hear to macon that I could send word to you how evry thing was geting on heare. Billy thommus came heare yestaday and today and tremed the box and heg. Tha looks very nice. The hayersons [hyacinths] is looking butafully. We hav had so much raine hear that we hav not dun much work in the garden. It was very cold hear last waek. We had a little snow stome last thursday but it did not last long. Thar has ben a grat meny cases of mesals and mumps in this plase all the wenter and I hav ben keeping the childran in the yard very close. It has bin all round us but we hav miss it this far. Littel miss millly Cobb has got the mumps now but it dos not hurt her a tall. I saw her this moning she was playing but her face was suelled a good del. Evry thing is looking very well on the lot. The grass that you had set out in the frunt yard is growing butafully. The old turkey gobbeler and hen is still at home tho a grat meny purssons are looseing thar turkeys. Tha dount seeme to be a tall arlarmed for david and Wag and jack are so sharp that tha are not alowed to reseve enny company at nith. I hav tow hens gon to seting under the old house. I dount no how menny eggs tha hav as the nest is ouet of my site. I hope I will hav sume spring chickens big or nuf to eate by the time you got home. The cow is douing very well for this time of the yar. She dount gave much milk tho ant vicey thinks she will sune go dry. The fodder gave oute and mr to[m] Craford bort a [load] of [illegible]. Socks the calf looks very well. Ant vicay hav ben trying her hand on sope. She mad sum very nice sope but it is soft for salt is so hard to find that she could not harden it. I had all the box that billy cut up bured after he had recset all that was missing. It was nice long peces and I though you wood want it saved.

Tel miss mary an that I made her a nice pincushun on her buth day. Plese mam when you rite to me send me sum derecttion a boute gardeing as I all was like to hav your derections so as [to] hav the things all nice. We are all well and send our best love to you and the childrn and all of the girls.

> your humble
> sirvant Aggy

[P.S.] my der mistess

Just as had finish my letter to you your moust wellcom letter came to hand. We all was vey glad to hear that you and childrn [are] well and mor then glad to hear that master tommy was trying to walk. Tha can be a plenty of ley sope got her[e] for ten cents but tarpentine sop is thirty cents and calico is from teenty five to thirty cents what littel thar is of it in Athns. Mr mors has moved his stor from hear to adlanta. Evry thing is very hy hear. We all are very glad that you left us so much beef to stand by. It is very nice and holds oute well. The turnups and collards are still holding oute. We all made the bacon hould oute as long as we coulod by take-ing a small pice at a time just to seeson the greens. We all sends you meny thanks for the ham that you gave us. The lard and syrup came today and I have loocked them up in the dairy and put the key a way. Ant vica and myself gos to charch on fast days and fest on prar and not cake.

Mary Ann Cobb to Howell Cobb

Macon, March 20, 1862

I had a letter from Aggy last week, all on our lot are well & all coming on smoothly. The two or three barrels of beef I salted down in Nov. & Dec. are holding out well, and Aggy says it is very nice. Aside from this they have to work to buy their meal and wood. Aggy takes in sewing. Ben works out by the day, and Vicey was to go out as a washerwoman by the day. All they can save from their support is their own. All I required of them was to take care of the house and lot—and the cow and calf and make me a garden in the Spring.

Mary Ann Cobb to Howell Cobb

Athens, May 17, 1863

Dr. Long[77] called today to see Aggy, who has violent cold, sore throat and headache.

Mary Ann Cobb to Howell Cobb

Athens, October 19, 1863

Tonight I packed & closed my silver chest, to be transferred to its pine case and thence to the Bank and that will be off my mind. . . . Aggy [is] in one corner of the dining room rubbing silver & jingling it to my agony.

---

77. Dr. Crawford Long (November 1, 1815–June 16, 1878), an Athens physician who is recognized as a pioneer in the use of anesthesia during surgery.

Mary Ann Cobb to "My Dear Son"

Athens, June 15, 1864

Captn Taylor has sold his little cottage home, no house in town, building negro houses in the country now. Isaac is helping. Shoes shop packed up and in status quo. Aggy says her house is too crowded for his tool box & bench. I tell her she had better be crowded by Isaac than the Yankees, while she has a choice.

Howell Cobb to Mary Ann Cobb

Macon, July 11, 1864

If Atlanta falls, I want you to leave Athens, and I still think, Baldwin is the best place for you to go to. I think the best arrangement is to send your valuables away, and leave yourself as soon as Atlanta falls. I would leave the house & lot in charge of Aggy, but if possible get some white person to occupy the house. I make these suggestions that you may be looking forward to a contingency, that I still think will not happen.

Mary Ann Cobb to Howell Cobb

Athens, [fall 1864]

What am [I] to do with Vicey, Melinda? Old Ben will go down with Mr. Moss to drive Captn R D B Taylor's horse & buggy. . . .

I shall take Angerona & Margret to Macon with me. Margret can cook for the family. . . .

Poor Aggy, it hurts me to have to leave her here not knowing what her fate may be if the Yankees overrun this upcountry. She may be starved to death, or dragged to the North.

Aggy Mills to Mary Ann Cobb

Athens, March 7, 1865

Dear Mistress

I write you a few lines as Mas Bajor is going down, and I would have written sooner but had no way of sending it. I know that you wish to hear from home as it is getting gardening time. I have hired an old man to work in the garden. He is a very nice gardener & I am going to try and have you a very good nice garden by the time you come home this summer. I am very glad to hear that you are coming home this summer. We all wish to see you very much. I am planting both gardens and if you have any particular directions to send you can let me know as I have just commenced planting. This has been a very hard winter and our corn gave out and I had to buy corn & potatoes with thread and chickens for Mr Ivy.[78] Mr Ivy is quite well and seems to be very well satisfied. I do everything I can to make him comfortable as possible. We are all tolerable well. The children has had the measles and I am afraid that they are taking the whooping cough. Elizas health is improving. All the rest are well. Give my love to all the children.

> Your humble servt
> Aggy

Howell Cobb to Mary Ann Cobb

Sumter County Plantations, September 15, 1865

I have got through making contracts with the negroes for the present year. . . . The poor creatures dont know their own mind. It would be as hard to get them to agree to go away, as it would be to get them to stay. . . . I think you had better keep Aggy until Christmas & longer if she is willing to stay. I doubt if you will be able to do as well. It will be difficult

---

78. Revered F. H. Ivey, pastor of Athens's First Baptist Church, was previously mentioned for having performed the marriage ceremony of Sylvia's daughter, Eliza, and William De Lyon. Mary Ann and two other Athenians had begun paying his salary, as the church was bereft of funds as a result of the disruptions caused by the war. Minutes of the First Baptist Church, June 3, 1865, and July 1, 1865, cited in Robert S. Gamble, "Athens: The Study of a Georgia Town during Reconstruction, 1865–1872" (master's thesis, University of Georgia, 1967), 22.

to get good servants for the next year. It may be better hereafter, when freedom has had its day, and the negroes have learned by experience what it is to be free.

Lamar Cobb to Mary Ann Cobb
Athens, February 9, 1866

I gave Aggy & Isaac their first months allowance, which amounted to a pretty heavy sum. Three & a half pounds[79] a week for her, Isaac, Lou . . . & half allowance for Fanny, but upon reflection I have determined to inform them that I shall give only one allowance for Fanny & Lou.

Mary Ann Lamar Cobb[80] to Mary Ann Cobb
Athens, March 13, 1867

I have been to see Aggie several times—you have no idea how nicely she is fixing your garden up (kitchen-garden). It looks neater than I ever saw it before. They have torn down all of the cottage except the middle rooms. Aggie is living in that until Edward repairs the rooms in the house opposite the kitchen for her use. The removal of the old house is going to be a great improvement to the lot but I hate to see it going on account of many childhood associations.

Mary Ann Cobb to John A. Cobb II
Athens, June 24, 1867

War & freedom have cleared the house of French China & Granite.[81] I am compelled to use my finest China every day, and to my horror and disgust I find Aggy sending the China plates to the Kitchen by Mrs Taylors

---

79. Lamar was referring to allotments of food, but it is not clear if he meant corn or pork or both.

80. Howell and Mary Ann's eldest daughter.

81. A type of mass-produced, everyday tableware.

Gipsy,[82] Charlotte. I stopped that, and hunted up the odd pieces of granite & French China to hand back & forth from the Kitchen. This will be kept up as long as I am here, but when I am absent, the China will begin to circulate among the darkies again. Oh Freedom! how many abuses have been committed in thy name—*Legions.*

Mary Ann Cobb to Howell Cobb

Athens, June 28, 1867

Usually I get down in time to breakfast with the school children, if I am tardy Sarah eats and hurrys to school before 8 o'clock. Then Anno,[83] I and occasionally Lizzie eat together while Howell, Mary and Mayon[84] breakfast when they are ready, one by one. I try to get Aggy to send their portions to the kitchen and give the servants their breakfast, but she gets wool gathering often & forgets my order, therefore there is *some* irregularity in the kitchen meals.

Aggy Mills to Mary Ann Cobb

Athens, [undated][85]

Dear Miss Maryann

I am very sorry that I will have to disappoint you today but I am sufring just like I was yesterday. But I hope to come friday. Please mam send me that money if you have it to spare just as much as you can spare and if I live I will work for you just as long as you wants me. Please excuse me as I am in need.

Yours truly Aggy Mills

---

82. "Gipsy" refers here to a scullery maid.

83. The family nickname for Andrew Cobb, Howell and Mary Ann's seventh son.

84. The family nickname for Mary Ann Lamar Cobb, Howell and Mary Ann's eldest daughter.

85. Given Aggy's unprecedented use of Mary Ann's first name, request for unpaid wages, decision to close the letter without pledging herself "your humble servant," and the absence of a mention of Aggy's "suffering" from an illness in any of Mary Ann's correspondence, it seems clear that this letter was written after 1867, probably sometime in the 1870s.

Epilogue

TELLING THE PAST IS SOMETIMES easier than walking through its traces. For all that the Cobb-Lamars owned in the nineteenth century, almost nothing remains in the twenty-first. Their plantation empire no longer exists. Other families now own their land and houses, unaware that the places were once connected to each other and to a larger history. Archived documents and heirloom furniture allow us a glimpse into that world but do not allow us to enter it. Access to the lives of the people they held in bondage is even more limited. Some, like Aggy and her daughters, or Sylvia and hers, spent their lives in proximity to the places in which they were enslaved, even after emancipation. Others, like Alfred and Berry, did not. Whether they stayed or moved along, geography took on a new importance in keeping some small communities alive and forming new ones as the network that had sustained them faded from existence. The problem for the historian, however, is that small communities based on geography and kinship rather than a complex vertical network do not leave robust archival trails. Time moves on, humans and their relationships fade from sight, and the traces disappear.

Like so many of their generation, every one of the people in this book must have been shocked by the speed and severity with which their world changed. The end of the Civil War ushered in a new age that challenged them all. For the Cobb-Lamar family it meant reckoning with the death and destruction the conflict had wrought. John B. died in battle while serving as a volunteer aide-de-camp to Howell during the 1862 Antietam campaign. His will bequeathed Swift Creek to his brother Andrew's daughter. Two years later, General William Tecumseh Sherman burned the Hurricane as he marched through Georgia, an act he justified as punishment of "one of the leading rebels of the South."[1] The family did not attempt to restore the plantation and eventually sold it. Howell died of a heart attack in October 1868, three months after President Andrew

---

1. William Tecumseh Sherman, *The Memoirs of General William T. Sherman* (1875; repr., Bloomington: University of Indiana Press, 1957), 185–86.

Johnson granted him a pardon for his role in secession and the war. Mary Ann survived for another two decades, but following the deaths of her brother and husband she turned the management of the family's plantations to her eldest son, John A. Cobb II. By the 1870s, the family's once-extensive agricultural empire no longer spanned the state and had contracted down to the remaining, but substantial, plantations in Sumter County. Within a few years, only the slightest vestiges of the old network remained, and those appear to have been fading rapidly.

The end of correspondence between John B., Howell, and Mary Ann in many ways terminated access to the human stories of those they once enslaved. The Cobb children employed hired servants to replace those who had died or moved away to seek opportunities elsewhere. These new servants appeared with far less frequency in their letters than those they had known in childhood and generally were discussed in terms of the quality of their labor rather than their connections to the family or a larger African American community.

With the simultaneous contraction of the Cobb-Lamar landholdings and the passing of an older generation, the network, which had previously bound an enslaved community that reached across Georgia, now gave way to small geographic clusters. Freedpeople once enslaved by the family remained connected to some others who came out of the same houses of bondage, but not all. Proximity was key. In Athens, Aggy and Isaac's community included their daughters, Louisa and Fanny, as well as Isaac's brother and sister-in-law, Edward and Martha Mills, and their children Isaac and Nancy. Nearby lived Sylvia and her daughter Polly, as well as a number of others they had labored beside for a lifetime, including Rachel's sons Bob and Laurence Cole. A similar community existed in Macon around the family of Aggy's brother, Robert Carter. Nearby, Ben Brewer, his wife Vicey, and their daughter Angeline lived in the same household as Malinda, another former Cobb household servant, and Loueza Lamar, who had been the head housekeeper in John B.'s home. Aggy's sister, Eliza Cobb, established her own family in Milledgeville. So too did Jenny Lamar and her husband, Bob, who were surrounded by their daughters, Clarissa and Lavinia, and numerous grandchildren. Becky Lamar, another of Jenny's daughters, remained in Sumter County at the center of a community that also included Alfred's parents, Abram and Hetty Putnam, and several of Berry's brothers and sisters.[2]

---

2. U.S. Census, 1870 and 1880, Clarke, Baldwin, Bibb, Sumter Counties, Georgia.

Because these small groups lived near one another and lost contact with those others who did not, they no longer needed formal methods of preserving their connections. Their stories and their voices had been inadvertently captured in deep, extended, and profoundly personal ways in decades of antebellum letters. Sadly, they are barely audible in a postbellum archive that captures them only rarely and in the smallest of fragments and at the shallowest of depths. Census and probate records show some few of them clustered together in geographic communities but reveal little of what they thought, felt, and experienced as they reckoned with the limits imposed on freedom and transformed a past dictated by others into futures of their own. The lines of communication that had once spanned the state—and hummed with news of enslaved family and friends, births and deaths, humor and tragedy—fell out of use and silent. Instead, countless new communities, defined by countless unremembered conversations, blossomed among free people who chose how and with whom to spend their lives.

Acknowledgments

RESEARCHING AND WRITING ABOUT networks of connectivity and support in the nineteenth century has made us especially aware how fortunate we are to have one of our own in the twenty-first. The webs that hold and sustain us are sometimes hard to see, and even harder to appreciate, but the experience of writing this book has been a reminder that we are always stronger together. This volume is the product of three friends sitting together at countless tables, in archives, coffee shops, and dining rooms. It was a lovely way to work. More importantly, we have benefited immensely from a circle of friends and mentors who were willing to spend meals, evenings, and weekends debating our evidence and refining our arguments. To all of them we owe great debts of thanks.

Larry Tenner enthusiastically took on the herculean task of creating the maps and genealogical charts that grace these pages. He took our ideas, researched deeply into nineteenth-century maps of Athens and Georgia, and built from scratch precise visual representations of the spaces inhabited by, and the familial connections between, the central personages of this book. The stunning simplicity of Larry's work is a testament to his intellect, drive, and enormous talent.

John C. Inscoe read multiple versions of the manuscript and, with generosity of spirit and seemingly endless goodwill, made extensive and insightful comments on each. Clay Capra spent his summer breaks assisting us with transcriptions and contributing research to footnotes. Mark Evans, TJ Kopcha, Melanie Pavich, Kiersten Rom, and Alexander M. Stephens spent years listening to bits of research and the developing narrative, then offered astute analysis and criticism as the book took shape. Milton Leathers, Charlotte Marshall, and Ben Brackett walked beside us and shared important stories, profound insights, and editorial advice as we dove deeply into archives, families, and houses they know intimately. Eric Arena, Bob Chambers, Jonathan Deen, Andrew Grodecki, Jeffry Netter, and Avis Williams offered personal and professional encouragement when we needed it most. Some of the most meaningful experiences we have had came as a result of working closely with dozens of students at Athens Academy, Putnam County Charter School System, and the University of Georgia, all of whom read and commented on portions of this manuscript, used some of the letters in their classes, and explored former Cobb-Lamar plantation and house sites with us.

None of our work would have been possible without the support of the leadership and staff of the Hargrett Rare Book and Manuscript Library at the University of Georgia. Toby Graham opened the door wide on the day we first suggested the project. Chuck Barber, Mazie Bowen, and Mary Linnemann have continued that good cheer and made our work possible over the years since. We are also deeply appreciative for the assistance provided by the staff of the Georgia Historical Society in Savannah and the Georgia Archives in Morrow. As research turned into writing, and at every long step since, we have been especially fortunate for the patient guidance of Mick Gusinde-Duffy at the University of Georgia Press and series editors Judkin Browning and Susanna Lee. Mick, Judkin, Susanna, and the anonymous readers who reviewed earlier drafts of this manuscript have made it much stronger than it otherwise would have been.

Finally, this volume is dedicated to our families. They have graciously given up parts of hours, days, and years because they have faith in us and believe in the importance of telling these stories. Thank you.

Index

New Perspectives on the Civil War Era

*Practical Strangers: The Courtship Correspondence of Nathaniel Dawson
and Elodie Todd, Sister of Mary Todd Lincoln*
EDITED BY STEPHEN BERRY AND ANGELA ESCO ELDER

*The Greatest Trials I Ever Had:
The Civil War Letters of Margaret and Thomas Cahill*
EDITED BY RYAN W. KEATING

*Prison Pens: Gender, Memory, and Imprisonment in the
Writings of Mollie Scollay and Wash Nelson, 1863–1866*
EDITED BY TIMOTHY J. WILLIAMS AND EVAN A. KUTZLER

*William Gregg's Civil War: The Battle to Shape
the History of Guerrilla Warfare*
EDITED AND ANNOTATED BY JOSEPH M. BEILEIN JR.

*Seen/Unseen: Hidden Lives in a
Community of Enslaved Georgians*
WRITTEN AND EDITED BY CHRISTOPHER R. LAWTON,
LAURA E. NELSON, RANDY L. REID

9 780820 358987